Book Love

Book Love:

A Celebration of Writers, Readers, and The Printed & Bound Book

....

Edited by James Charlton & Bill Henderson

Introduction by Bill Henderson

THE LITERARY COMPANION SERIES

PUSHCART

ISBN: 978-1-888889-61-1

Pushcart Press
P.O. Box 380
Wainscott, New York 11975

Distributed by W.W. Norton Co.
500 Fifth Avenue
New York, New York 10110

Designed by Mary Kornblum, CMYK DESIGN INC.
Layout by Jeffrey Stern, CMYK DESIGN INC.

With special thanks to Williams Cole, Meaghan Beasley, Mary Sheldon,
Priscilla Potter, Eileen Obser, Marilyn Abel, S. Dianne Moritz, Blythe Heppe
and Genie Henderson

Thanks to the Trustees of the Boston Public Library and the New York
Public Library

PRINTED IN THE UNITED STATES OF AMERICA

For Wendell Berry

PRELUDE

....

Things are in the saddle / and ride mankind.
RALPH WALDO EMERSON

BOOK LOVE is a love letter from hundreds of writers and readers and their friends to the printed and bound book. We hear the book is in trouble. The e-reader is taking over like an invasive weed or a mutant carp.

This recent onslaught of e-readers was announced with a veneer of the best of intentions. The book needed improving, said one maven, who also sells diapers and soup on line. An MIT visionary predicted that in five years we will read almost no paper books – just digital devices. The book would become a relic, a collector's item, the e-experts agreed. And of course with the death of the book our bookstores and libraries would wither and die.

Said the e-experts, in the future all info and literature would be available on the device of the moment (sure to be replaced by the device of the next moment). You may never have to leave the comfort of home or bed. The latest best seller – indeed millions of out-of-print books (you didn't know you needed that many) could be had at the click of a button. This was billed as an improvement.

Lots of people are making lots of money and telling us this is for our own good. Twittering away, we never stop to think. In fact, we may be losing the ability to think.

Nicholas Carr in his *The Shallows: What the Internet Is Doing To Our Brains* (Norton, 2010) notes that his friends, after years of digital addiction, can't read in depth anymore. Their very brains are changing, physically. They are becoming "chronic scatterbrains...even a blog post of more than 3 or 4 paragraphs is too much to absorb."

Carr continues: "For the last five centuries, ever since Gutenberg made reading a popular pursuit, the linear, literary mind has been at the center of art, science and society. As supple as it is subtle, it's been the imaginative mind of the Renaissance, the rational mind of the Enlightenment, the inventive mind of the Industrial Revolution, even the subversive mind of Modernism. It may soon be yesterday's mind."

Because our brains can no longer think beyond a twitter, we can't write well. And we can't read well either. The idea of reading—let alone writing—*War and Peace, Bleak House* or *Absalom, Absalom!*—is fading into an impossible dream.

In any case, what serious writer would create exclusively for an e-reader? It's like farting into the wind. Writers hope, mostly in vain, that their work will endure for a few years or even centuries, in handsome printed and bound volumes. Why bother at all if your words are to be digitized into instantly accessible and disposable battery dependent gas?

• • •

Some think that the e-reader will save trees. Soon, according to the *New York Times* of January 3, 2011, we will possess over one hundred million e-readers. What a saving in our forests, right? Wrong.

Here's what an e-reader is. A battery operated slab, about a pound, one half-inch thick, perhaps an aluminum border, rubberized back, plastic, metal, silicon, a bit of gold, plus rare metals such as columbite-tantalite (Google it) ripped from the earth, often in war-torn Africa. To make one e-reader requires 33 pounds of minerals, plus 79 gallons of water to produce the battery and printed writing and refine the minerals. The production of other e-reading devices such as cell phones, iPads and whatever new gizmo will pop up (and down) in the years ahead is similar.

"The adverse health impacts from making one e-reader are estimated to be 70 times greater than those for making a single book," says the *Times*.

Then you figure that the one hundred million e-readers will be outmoded in short order – to be replaced by one hundred million new and improved devices in the years ahead that will likewise be replaced by new models *ad infinitum*, and you realize an environmental disaster is at hand. We will have lost a chunk of our planet as we lose our minds to the digital juggernaut.

Here's what it takes to make a book, which, if it is any good, will be shared by many readers and preserved and appreciated in personal, public and university libraries that survive the gigantic digital book burning: recycled paper, a dash of minerals and two gallons of water. Batteries not necessary. If trees are harvested they can be replanted.

The *Times* concludes (April 4, 2010), "The most ecologically virtuous way to read a book starts by walking to your local library."

• • •

This little book came about over three decades. In 1978, my co-editor and friend Jim Charlton put together a pamphlet of quotations about writing and distributed it at the American Booksellers Convention. Jim and I decided to expand it with more quotes and published it as the *Writer's Quotation Book* the next year. It went through four editions and became a bible for writers. Later, Steven Gilbar's *Reader's Quotation Book* – a hymn to the reader – joined Pushcart's "literary companion" series. You will find a sampling of the best quotations from each book in the 600 plus selections that follow.

Back in those days, a good writer was held in respect. He or she was not denigrated as a "content provider". The reader too was respected, was not a mere "consumer" (hideous word). And books were designated solely by title not by ISBN number and publishers did not call them "units" but books. Imagine!

Somewhere in the last four decades extreme avarice invaded book publishing. In the mid-seventies Mattel toys attempted to snatch Random House. The toy folks saw profits in print and soon other conglomerates demanded bucks from books. Editors and publishing companies that didn't rake in the cash were fired, sold or liquidated.

That books would ever be seen as a profit opportunity is rather funny. Most books – about 80% of them – lose money. A few best-sellers might make up for these losses but book publishing is not where one turns for a gigantic payday – the kind demanded by our "greed is good" hustlers.

Then along came the e-reader and other devices. Huge profits were envisioned by the gadget gurus. And on we flew into chaos.

• • •

BOOK LOVE is published for those who still love books, who hope like Jonathan Lethem that books are "unkillable" and agree with Jason Epstein that "actual books will continue to be the irreplaceable repository of our collective wisdom". The authors of the quotations that follow say all of this better than we ever could. Books are our history and our future. If they survive, we will too. Books, readers, writers – on this trinity we keep the faith.

Finally perhaps the book's best defense is that the printed and bound volume is seductive. Metal, silicon, glass and columbite-tantalite can never touch the sexy book. Try to curl up with an e-reader or take a bath with one. Here's the late Jerome Stern, in his R-rated testimony reprinted from *Minutes of the Lead Pencil Club* (Pushcart Press, 1996). Few have said it better.

> I have just come from an exhibition that told me that books will be replaced by electronic libraries...with thousands of

volumes, gigabytes of memory dancing on pixilated screens at which we will blearily stare into eternity.

And so in the face of the future I must sing this song of the book. Nothing more voluptuous do I know than sitting with bright pictures, fat upon my lap and turning glossy pages of giraffes and Gauguins, penguins and pyramids...

I love heavy dictionaries, their tiny pictures, complicated columns, minute definitions of incarnative and laniary, hagboat and fopdoodle.

I love the texture of pages, the high gloss slickness of magazines as slippery as oiled eels, the soft nubile of old books, delicate India paper, so thin my hands tremble trying to turn the fluttering dry leaves, and the yellow, cheap, coarse paper of mystery novels so gripping that I don't care that the plane circles Atlanta forever...

I love the feel of ink on the paper, the shiny varnishes, the silky lacquers, the satiny mattes.

I love the press of letters on thick paper, the roughness sizzles my fingers with centuries of craft embedded in pulped old rags, my hands caress the leather of old bindings crumbling like ancient gentlemen.

The books I hold for their heft, to riff their pages, to smell their smoky dustiness the rise of time in my nostrils.

I love bookstores, a perfect madness of opportunity, a lavish feast eaten by walking up aisles and as fast as my hand reaches out...

I sing these pleasures of white paper and black ink, of the small jab of the hard cover at the edge of my diaphragm, of the look of type, of the flip of a page, the sinful abandon of the turned down corner, the reckless possessiveness of my marginal scroll, the cover picture as much a part of the book as the contents itself.

And I also love those great fat Bibles evangelists wave like otter pelts, the long graying sets of unreadable authors, the tall books of babyhood enthusiastically crowned, the embossed covers of adolescence, the tiny poetry anthologies you could slip in your packet and the yellowing cookbooks of recipes for glace blanche dupont and Argentine mocha toast, their stains and spots souvenirs of long evenings full of love and argument, and the talk, like as not, of books, books, books.

• • •

World without end. Amen. Amen.

B.H.

Books

I cannot remember a time when I was not in love with them—with the books themselves, cover and binding and the paper they were printed on, with their smell and their weight and with their possession in my arms, captured and carried off to myself.

EUDORA WELTY

Please, no matter how we advance technology please don't abandon the book—there is nothing in our material world more beautiful than the book.

PATTI SMITH *after winning the 2010 National Book Award*

For flexibility and long term data storage, nothing comes close to the book. The announcement of the death of the book as pronounced by pessimists, oligarchs and those who ought to know better is premature.

RICK MOODY

A book is not only a friend, it makes friends for you. When you have possessed a book with mind and spirit, you are enriched. But when you pass it on you are enriched threefold.

HENRY MILLER

If you believe, as I do, that your *work* is the footsteps you leave in the sands of time, then every book you publish should contain the proof of that devotional promise.

DAVID R. GODINE, *publisher*

It is a great thing to start life with a small number of really good books, which are your very own.

SIR ARTHUR CONAN DOYLE

A good book is the best of friends, the same today and forever.

MARTIN FARAQUHAR TUPPER

A book is like a sailboat or a bicycle, in that it's a perfect invention. I don't care what series number of Kindle you're on, it is never going to be better than the book.

RICHARD HOWORTH, *Square Books*

Some folks think e-books will kill the hardcover, but I think the mass market is more at risk—it's a short jump from disposable to virtual.

DANIEL GOLDIN, *Boswell Book Company*

Lord! When you sell a man a book you don't sell just twelve ounces of paper and ink and glue—your sell him a whole new life. Love and friendship and humour and ships at sea by night— there's all heaven and earth in a book, a real book.

CHRISTOPHER MORLEY

I find television to be very educating. Every time somebody turns on the set, I go in the other room and read a book.

GROUCHO MARX

The best of a book is not the thought which it contains, but the thought which it suggests; just as the charm of music swells not in the tones but in the echoes of our hearts.

OLIVER WENDELL HOLMES

A book is the only place in which you can examine a fragile thought without breaking it, or explore an explosive idea without fear it will go off in your face. It is one of the few havens remaining where a man's mind can get both provocation and privacy.

EDWARD P. MORGAN

Hundreds and thousands of people flock to book festivals...they cherish the book. And they believe this is an artifact they want in their lives.

JOHN B. THOMPSON, *Merchants of Culture*

It is rectangular and thick, heavy enough to stop a bullet or press a leaf flat. It will, you think, never let you through. And then you begin to lean into it... and you're in. You're in the book.

NICHOLSON BAKER

There is no Frigate like a Book
To take us Lands away
Nor any Coursers like a Page
Of prancing Poetry—

EMILY DICKINSON

The book, if you would see anything in it, requires to be read in the clear, brown twilight atmosphere in which it was written; if opened in the sunshine, it is apt to look exceedingly like a volume of blank pages.
NATHANIEL HAWTHORNE

The world of books is the most remarkable creation of man. Nothing else that he builds ever lasts, monuments fall, nations perish, civilizations grow old and die out, and after an era of darkness new races build others. But in the world of books are volumes that have seen this happen again and again and yet live on, still young, still as fresh as the day they were written, still telling men's hearts, of the hearts of men centuries dead.
CLARENCE DAY

When things get tense in a book, you start doing things like stroking the edge of the pages. When you do that on your iPhone, the next thing you know you've frozen the thing.
SARAH McNALLY, *McNally Jackson Books*

I love books—the kind that, when you open them at a yard sale table, souvenirs from somebody else's life flutter out like freed birds, the kind that get passed around among friends and family.
PATRICIA FRISELLA

Ancient and weighty, in its worn leather coat,
The Dictionary
held its tongue,
refusing to reveal its secrets
PABLO NERUDA

How distinctly, in after years, one remembers the feel of a favorite book, the typography, the binding, the illustrations and so on. How easily one can localize the time and place of the first reading.
HENRY MILLER

Books allow for a soulfulness that screens, with their jumpy impersonality, cannot duplicate—any more than the movies can duplicate the intimate intensity of a theater.
ADAM GOPNIK

I cannot live without books.
THOMAS JEFFERSON

Outside of a dog, a book is a man's best friend. Inside of a dog it's too dark to read.
GROUCHO MARX

I would be most content if my children grew up to be the kind of people who think decorating consists mostly of building enough bookshelves.
ANNA QUINDLEN

Always read something that will make you look good if you die in the middle of it.

P.J. O'ROURKE

A book reads the better which is our own, and has been so long known to us, that we know the topography of its blots, and dog's ears, and can trace the dirt in it to having read it at tea with buttered muffins.

CHARLES LAMB

I know every book of mine by its smell, and I have but to put my nose between the pages to be reminded of all sorts of things.

GEORGE GISSING

I miss library card catalogs terribly, and I hate searching for books using the on-line catalog. Reading books on a computer seems like having one's hand cut off (Ray Bradbury says that he wrote Fahrenheit 451 in a library, and that he frequently dashed into the stack to open books and smell them for inspiration).

JILL CARPENTER

The dark side of the information technology explosion is that it will breed a population that believes nothing and, perhaps even more dangerous, a population ready to believe only one "truth" fanatically and willing to kill for.

ALVIN TOFFLER

Americans are suckers for utopian promises. They have been ever since the Puritans invented the idea of radical newness, in the 17th century. We will look back on what is now claimed for the information superhighway and wonder how we ever psyched ourselves into believing all that bulldust about social fulfillment through interface and connectivity. But by then we will have some other fantasy to chase, its approaches equally lined with entrepreneurs and flacks, who will be its main beneficiaries.

ROBERT HUGHES

Every time we take away a technology, we find a gift underneath.

SCOTT SAVAGE, *Plain*

Gutenberg (hesitantly): Perhaps the book, like God, is an idea some men will cling to. The revolution of print pursued a natural course. Like a river, print flowed to its readers, and the cheapness of the means permitted it, where the channel was narrow, to trickle. This electronic flood you describe has no banks; it massively delivers but what to whom? There is something intrinsically small about its content, compared to the genius of its working. And—if I may point out a technical problem— its product never achieves autonomy from its means of delivery. A book can lie unread for a century, and all it needs to come to life is to be scanned by a literate brain.

JOHN UPDIKE

Attend any conference on telecommunications or computer technology, and you will be attending a celebration of innovative machinery that generates, stores, and distributes more information, more conveniently, at greater speeds than ever before. To the questions "What problem does the information solve?" the answer is usually "How to generate, store, and distribute more information, more conveniently, at greater speeds than ever before."

NEIL POSTMAN

The [digital] present is more frightening than any imaginable future I might dream up. If Marshall McLuhan were alive today, he'd have a nervous breakdown.

WILLIAM GIBSON

The oversell on the "information superhighway" exploits the same public gullibility that true atomic-energy believers exploited decades ago. It's a gullibility that flows from a touchingly credulous eagerness to believe that new miracle ages are constantly lurking just around the corner.

RUSSELL BAKER

I think, that fiction, poetry, and essays on the Net are heading toward the status of junk mail.

W. SCOTT OLSEN

Every other week someone says that books are dead or dying, that just around the corner is the black hour when they will be curiosities like stereopticon slides or milk stools—probably the same thing they said when radio was invented, when television flickered its way into our living rooms.

ANNIE PROULX

I just don't personally believe in reading novels on a screen. There's a lot of content that's now being delivered on paper that's fine on paper.

OLAF OLAFSSON, *President, Sony Electronic Publishing*

After Star Wars and its sequels made hundreds of millions of dollars, the filmmaker George Lucas built himself a self-contained, state-of the-art studio with all the most advanced special-effect technology. The core of this studio, both architecturally and spiritually, according to Lucas himself is the books in his library.

JOE DAVID BELLAMY

People go into book publishing and bookselling because they want to be involved with words and books. They don't want to make money. Those technology people are in love with games, in love with computers, and in love with making money. They have no problem talking about units.

MICHAEL LYNTON, *former Senior Vice President,*
Walt Disney Publishing Company

It seems to me the book has not just aesthetic values—the charming little clothy box of the thing, the smell of the glue, even the print. Which has its own beauty. But there's something about the sensation of ink on paper that is in some sense a thing, a phenomenon rather than an epiphenomenon. I can't break the association of electric trash with the screen. Words on the screen give the sense of being just another passing electronic wiggle.

JOHN UPDIKE

For several days after my first book was published I carried it about in my pocket, and took surreptitious peeps at it to make sure the ink had not faded.

SIR JAMES M. BARRIE

I am very foolish over my own book. I have a copy, which I constantly read and find very illuminating. Swift confesses to something of the sort with his own compositions.

J.B. YEATS

I don't keep any copy of my books around.... They would embarrass me. When I finish writing my books, I kick them in the belly, and have done with them.

LUDWIG BEMELMANS

The virtues of a book are independent of any bells, whistles or animation it might be made to contain.

ADAM GOPNIK

There's something special about people who are interested in the printed word. They are a species all their own—learned, kind, knowledgeable and human.

NATHAN PINE, *bookseller*

Sir, the fact that a book is in the public library brings no comfort. Books are the one element in which I am personally and nakedly acquisitive. If it weren't for the law I would steal them. If it weren't for my purse I would buy them.

HAROLD LASKI

Never lend books. For no one ever returns them; the only books I have in my library are books that other folk have lent me.

ANATOLE FRANCE

Your borrowers of books—those mutilators of collections, spoilers of the symmetry of shelves, and creators of odd volumes.

CHARLES LAMB

When I get a little money, I buy books; and if any is left, I buy food and clothes.

DESIDERIUS ERASMUS

Hard-covered books break up friendships. You loan a hard-covered book to a friend and when he doesn't return it you get mad at him. It makes you mean and petty. But twenty-five cent books are different.

JOHN STEINBECK

The multitude of books is making us ignorant.
VOLTAIRE

A book is like a garden carried in the pocket.
CHINESE PROVERB

There is a good saying to the effect that when a new book
appears one should read an old one. As an author I would
not recommend too strict an adherence to this saying.
WINSTON CHURCHILL

One old lady who wants her head lifted wouldn't be so
bad, but you multiply her two hundred and fifty thousand
times and what you get is a book club.
FLANNERY O'CONNOR

There is nothing so important as the book can be.
MAXWELL PERKINS

All that Mankind has done, thought gained or been: it is
lying as in magic preservation in the pages of books. They
are the chosen possession of man.
THOMAS CARLYLE

The walls of books around him, dense with the past,
formed a kind of insulation against the present world and
its disasters.
ROSS MACDONALD

A room without books is like a body without soul.
CICERO

Books are a delightful society. If you go into a room filled with books, even without taking them down from their shelves, they seem to speak to you, to welcome you.

WILLIAM E. GLADSTONE

There are books which I love to see on the shelf. I feel a virtue goes out of them, but I should think it undue familiarity to read them.

SAMUEL McCHORD CROTHERS

As good almost kill a man as kill a good book: who kills a man kills a reasonable creature, God's image; but he who destroys a good book kills reason itself, kills the image of God, as it were, in the eye.

JOHN MILTON

An ordinary man can surround himself with two thousand books and have at least one place in the world in which it is possible to be happy.

AUGUSTINE BIRRELL

Just the knowledge that a good book is waiting one at the end of a long day makes that day happier.

KATHLEEN NORRIS

If you cannot read all your books, at any rate handle, or as it were, fondle them—peer into them, let them fall open where they will, read from the first sentence that arrests the eye, set them back on the shelves with your own hands, arrange them on your own plan so that you at least know where they are. Let them be your friends; let them at any rate be your acquaintances.

WINSTON CHURCHILL

Americans like fat books and thin women.

RUSSELL BAKER

Everything in the world exists to end up in a book.

STÉPHANE MALLARMÉ

It's not that screens are bad and books are good, but what books do depends on the totality of what they are... above all the way they invite a child to withdraw from this world into a world alongside ours in an activity at once mentally strenuous and physically still.

ADAM GOPNIK

Books have saved my life more than once. I was driving a Morris Minor van along a windy dark road slick with rain. I misjudged a bad bend, went through the windshield and the engine sheared from its mountings and broke into the cab. It would have cut off one leg had I not been carrying the complete works of Shakespeare on my knee.

JEANETTE WINTERSON

I like how the library smells. Close your eyes and remember it: musty, dusty, gluey, eternal. I like to suck in a lungful of this book-sweet aroma, pick out a volume that has been kneaded by a hundred hands, then go read it under a tree.
LEE EISENBERG

As a child I felt that books were holy objects, to be caressed, rapturously sniffed, and devotedly provided for. 1 gave my life to them—I still do. 1 continue to do what 1 did as a child: dream of books, make books, and collect books.
MAURICE SENDAK

And how I felt it beat
Under my pillow, in the morning's dark,
An hour before the sun would let me read!
My books!
ELIZABETH BARRETT BROWNING

Literature illuminates life only for those to whom books are a necessity. Books are unconvertible assets, to be passed on only to those who possess them already.
ANTHONY POWELL

Blessings be the inventor of the alphabet, pen and printing press! Life would be—to me in all events—a terrible thing without books.
L. M. MONTGOMERY

He did not think of these books as something invented to beguile the idle hour, but as living creatures, caught in the very behaviour of living—surprised behind their misleading severity of form and phrase. He was eavesdropping upon the past, being let into the great world that had plunged and glittered and sumptuously sinned long before little Western towns were dreamed of.

WILLA CATHER

Sir, he hath never fed on the dainties that are bred in a book; he hath not eat paper, as it were; he hath not drunk ink; his intellect is not replenished; he is only an animal, only sensibled in the duller parts.

WILLIAM SHAKESPEARE *(Love's Labours Lost)*

We'd go for walks and picnics, taking books in baskets, and sit under trees and read. I now live once more in the same part of the country which isn't much changed since I was a child; I can still find the spot where David Copperfield first met Mr. Murdstone and the tree where the Knight of the Leopard had his picnic with Saladin.

JOAN AIKEN

Ordinary books are like meteors. Each of them has only one moment, a moment when it soars screaming like the phoenix, all its pages aflame. For that single moment we love them ever after, although they soon turn to ashes. With bitter resignation we sometimes wander late at night through the extinct pages that tell their stone dead messages like wooden rosary beads.

BRUNO SCHULZ *(The Book)*

....

Remember
First to possess his books; for without them
He's but a sot, as I am.

WILLIAM SHAKESPEARE *(The Tempest)*

Books are as lively, and as vigorously productive, as those
fabulous dragon's teeth: and being sown up and down,
may chance to spring up armed men.

JOHN MILTON

Books are not only titles on their author's monuments, but
epitaphs, preserving their memories, be they good, or bad,
beyond short lived pyramids, or mausoleum piles of stone.

RICHARD WHITLOCK

Books are yours,
Within whose silent chambers treasure lies
Preserved from age to age; more precious far
Than that accumulated store of gold
And orient gems which, for a day of need,
The sultan hides deep in ancestral tombs,
These hoards of truth you can unlock at will.

WILLIAM WORDSWORTH

The writings of the wise are the only riches our posterity
cannot squander.

WALTER SAVAGE LANDOR

It is with books as with men, a very small number play a
great part: the rest are confounded with the multitude.

VOLTAIRE

....

Without the word, without the writing of books, there is no history, there is no concept of humanity. And if anyone wants to try to enclose in a small space, in a single house or a single room, the history of the human spirit and to make it his own, he can only do this in the form of a collection of books.

HERMANN HESSE

Whoever touches a book touches not only "a man" but Man. Man is the animal who weeps and laughs—and writes. If the first Prometheus brought fire from heaven in a fennel-stalk, the last will take it back—in a book.

JOHN COWPER POWYS

And books! those miraculous memories of high thoughts and golden moods; those silver shells, tremulous with the wonderful secrets of the ocean of life; those love-letters that pass from hand to hand of a thousand lovers that never meet.

RICHARD LE GALLIENNE

Books precede and outlast us. They are cemeteries of the living. The solemn buckram sepulchers contain the wildest of life, and the carousing corpses within—begot by an author, realized by a printer, first freed by a paperknife—now wait only for sight to fall on their pages for them to rise up and live.

PAUL THEROUX

The book, with its intimacy, its forcibility, its accessibility, its freedom from outside energy sources, its ability to reach into tyrannic countries, and be hidden under mattresses, and be smuggled in the false bottoms of suitcases—all these are great advantages.

DANIEL BOORSTIN

You will find then in the libraries of the most arrant idlers all that orators or historians have written—bookcases built up as high as the ceiling. Nowadays a library takes rank with a bathroom as a necessary ornament of a house. I could forgive such ideas, if they were due to extravagant desire for learning. As it is, these productions of men whose genius we revere, paid for at a high price, with their portraits ranged in line above them, are got together to adorn and beautify a wall.

LUCIUS ANNAEUS SENECA

I think it is good that books still exist, but they make me sleepy.

FRANK ZAPPA

I believe books will never disappear. It is impossible for it to happen. Of all mankind's diverse tools, undoubtedly the most astonishing are his books.... If books were to disappear, history would disappear. So would men.

JORGE LUIS BORGES

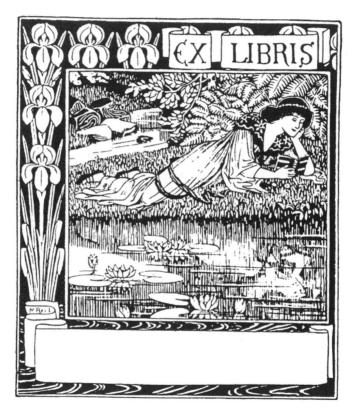

A book collector is like a lighthouse keeper who offers sanctuary to buffeted and exhausted migrants as they home towards the friendly beam. Once behind glass they are safe from pollution.

CYRIL CONNOLLY

To compensate a little for the treachery and weakness of my memory I have adopted the habit for some time now of adding at the end of each book the time I finished reading it and the judgment I have derived of it as a whole, so that this may represent to me at least the sense and general idea I had conceived of the author in reading it.

MICHEL DE MONTAIGNE

What a pity it is that all owners of books do not put their signatures on a fly-leaf. Our predecessors in proprietorship shared our tastes, and if they had taken the trouble to write their names, they might receive from us, and we from them, a slight telepathic impact of a friendly character.

ANDREW LANG

Like the faces of human beings, books develop character as they age. Is there a more pleasant room in a house than a library, a jungle more filled with adventure than a second-hand bookstore?

ERIK CHRISTIAN HAUGAARD

If a book is worth reading, it is worth buying. No book is worth anything which is not worth much; nor is it serviceable until it has been read, and re-read, and loved, and loved again.

JOHN RUSKIN

Your books take on something of your personality, and your environment also—you know a second-hand book sometimes is so much more flesh and blood than a new one—and it is almost terrible to think that your ideas, yourself in your books, may be giving life to generations of readers after you are forgotten.

T. E. LAWRENCE

One cannot begin too soon to buy one's own books, if for no other reason...than the freedom which they give to use their fly-leaves for your own private index of those matters in their pages which are particularly yours, whether for interest, or information, or for what not—those things which the index makers never by any possibility include.

JOHN LIVINGSTON LOWES

You can't read a book without thinking about the origins of those little characters we call type. They were designed to express a thought, an idea; and placed next to each other, they might change the world—as they often have. The typeface chosen should reflect the book's content, contribute to the clarity of the ideas expressed, and be read with ease. Like notes in a musical score, those letters should cling to you, continue to grow in your mind, and develop understanding and sensitivity—a sense of the quality of life.

FRITZ EICHENBERG

Books also had a meaning for her as physical objects: she loved to walk down the street with a book under her arm. It had the same significance for her as an elegant cane for the dandy a century ago. It differentiated her from others.

MILAN KUNDERA *(The Unbearable Lightness of Being)*

Books perfume and give weight to a room, which without books suffers from amnesia. A bookcase is as good as a view, as much of a panorama as the sight of a city or a river. There are dawns and sunsets in books—storms, fogs, zephyrs.

ANATOLE BROYARD

A precious—mouldering pleasure—'tis—
To meet an Antique Book—
In just the Dress his Century wore—
A privilege—I think—

EMILY DICKINSON

Demoyte's books were all behind glass, so that the room was full of reflections. Demoyte was a connoisseur of books. Spotless, gilded and calved, books to be held gently in the hand and admired, and which recalled to mind the fact that a book is a thing and not just a collection of thoughts.

IRIS MURDOCH *(The Sandcastle)*

[Douglas Jerrold] had an almost reverential fondness for books—books themselves—and said he could not bear to treat them, or see them treated, with disrespect. He told us it gave him pain to see them turned on their faces, stretched open, or dog's-eared, or carelessly flung down, or in any way misused.

GERALD & MARY COWDEN CLARKE

I could make a stack and see them a few feet away as a pyramid of print... a Pennine of pages. They appeared to me as stepping-stones to some state that I didn't know about.

ALAN SILLITOE

There was a time when I really did love books—loved the sight and smell and feel of them, I mean, at least if they were fifty or more years old. Nothing pleased me quite so much as to buy a job lot of them for a shilling at a country auction. There is a peculiar flavor about the battered unexpected books you pick up in that kind of collection.

GEORGE ORWELL

If I were rich I would have many books, and I would pamper myself with bindings bright to the eye and soft to the touch, paper generously opaque, and type such as men designed when printing was very young. I would dress my gods in leather and gold, and burn candles of worship before them at night, and string their names like beads on a rosary.

WILL DURANT

I am consumed with enthusiasm for books, as with disgust for all things else.

CICERO

A true bibliophile is a lover in every sense of the work. You have to sleep with the book, to live with the book. You must handle the book, you must not be afraid to have intimate contact with the book.

PIERRE BESÈS, *bookseller*

When I get offered a book, I see it, I feel it, I browse through it. I smell it. I get in touch with it. And then I buy it. Or I don't buy it.

HERIBERT TENSCHERT, *bookseller*

This is how you know a rare book when you see one. You feel an electric tingling running through your fingers... Fingerspitzengefuhl.

LEONA ROSTENBERG, *scholar/bookseller*

I have given my friends to understand that when I am done with this earth certain of my books shall be buried with me.

EUGENE FIELD, *19th century author/bookseller*

To a true collector the acquisition of an old book is a rebirth. This is the childlike element which in a collector mingles with the element of old age.

WALTER BENJAMIN

The [bibliomaniac's] tales of acquisition and success brings to mind the activities of the hypersexual male hysteric who must constantly reassure himself that he has not been castrated. It seems germane to this point that Casanova settled down as a librarian.

DR. NORMAN WEINER, *psychoanalyst*

You can never be too thin, too rich, or have too many books.

CARTER BURDEN

There are librarians who say to me "Why do you want to be in books anyway? Everything is going to go electronic." I say nobody cuddles you like your mother in bed with a book.

LLOYD E. COTSEN, *children's book collector*

The true university of these days is a collection of books.

THOMAS CARLYLE

The more a book is read, if it's read to death even, that's what I love. What moves me beyond words is that there have been people here before me, and now I am joining their company.

JAY FLEIGELMAN

Federigo da Montefeltro, the second duke of Urbino (1422–1482) built an exceptional library of magnificently bound manuscripts that was famous in its time for excluding printed books as inferior substitutes.

NICHOLAS A. BASBANES

Good books do not waste our time as most people do; books are friends which enrich us as much as we desire.

CARDINAL AUGUSTIN VALIER

What bothers me above all else is that a public institution will vandalize itself and decide it will spend, if not waste, huge amounts of money for technology, and at the same time dispose of an existing book collection that is irreplaceable. It is a hate crime directed at the past.

NICHOLSON BAKER

I began my life as I shall no doubt end it: amidst books. In my grandfather's study there were books everywhere. It was forbidden to dust them, except once a year. Though I did not yet know how to read I already revered those standing stones.

JEAN-PAUL SARTRE

My students love, they don't just like, they love their books. And the ones who are the most skilled are most often the ones who are lovers of traditional books.

ANTHONY GRAFTON, *Princeton University*

A premium is placed on one's ability to communicate in short bursts. Celebrities rise to prominence and then disappear very quickly. The disposable syndrome has moved from paper plates, diapers, and clothes to information.

KENNETH DOWLIN, *The Electronic Library*

My mother died surrounded by her friends and her family and her books.

> JOHN F. KENNEDY, JR., *on the death of his mother, Jacqueline*

It is the essential character of our time that the triumph of the lie, the mutilation of culture, and the persecution of the word no longer shock us into anger.

> FELIX FRANKFURTER

The heads of houses are, in general, people who came up through marketing or sales, not through editorial and certainly not through production. They may possibly know the difference between a headband and a foot margin, but it is unlikely. Their mission is not the manufacturing of a durable and handsome product but the making of profits for the company. They are, as they probably need to be, executives and administrators and corporate functionaries, but they are not book people.

> DAVID R. GODINE, *publisher*

Old fashioned books may fade or decay; but the technology for human access to their contents, so long as they survive, has not changed since the invention of the spectacles.

> SIR ANTHONY KEMY

No collector or lover of books ever possesses a great book or manuscript until it possesses him

> FREDERICK R. GOFF

....

Pray ponder for a moment to fully appreciate the rarity and importance of this precious consignment from the Old to the New World. It is not only the first Bible, but a fine copy of the First Book ever printed. Let none of Uncle Sam's Custom House officials see it without first reverentially lifting their hats.

HENRY STEVENS, *bookseller, on the arrival of a*
Biblia Latina in New York

He scarcely ate, he no longer slept, but he dreamed whole days and nights of his fixed idea: books.

GUSTAVE FLAUBERT, *in Bibliomania*

The sight of the cover of a book one has previously read retains, woven into the letters of its title, the moonbeams of a far-off summer night.

MARCEL PROUST

Books, books, books in all their aspects, in form and spirit, their physical selves and what reading releases from their hieroglyphic pages, in their sight and smell, in their touch and feel to the questing hand, and in the intellectual music which they sing to thoughtful brain and loving heart, books are to me the best of all symbols, the realest of all reality.

LAWRENCE CLARK POWELL

The man who puts his hand on some precious, rare, lovable or at least, seemly volume, and who does not press it with a hand both gentle and firm, who does not voluptuously pass a tender palm over its back, its sides, and its edges, that man never had the instinct that makes Groliers and Doubles.

ANATOLE FRANCE

There's so much more to a book than just reading. I've seen children play with books, fondle books, smell books, and that's every reason why books should be lovingly produced.

MAURICE SENDAK

One may have any kind of music he chooses; it is only a question of mood. There is no deep harmony, no haunting melody, ever heard by the spirit of man which one may not hear if he knows his book thoroughly.

HAMILTON WRIGHT MABIE

Your house, being the place in which you read, can tell us the position books occupy in your life, if they are a defense you set up to keep the outside world at a distance, if they are a dream into which you sink as if into a drug, or bridges you cast toward the outside, toward the world that interests you so much that you want to multiply and extend its dimensions through books.

ITALO CALVINO

How I loved the authors of my books; how I loved them too, not only for the imaginative pleasures they afforded me, but for their making me love the very books themselves, and delight to be in contact with them.

LEIGH HUNT

Books are not made for furniture, but there is nothing else that so beautifully furnishes a house. The plainest row of books that cloth or paper ever covered is more significant of refinement than the most elaborately carved etagere or sideboard.

HENRY WARD BEECHER

To treat books as furniture is at any rate a better use for them than reading them; moreover it concerns the book as a material object. It deals with the outside of books which, ninety-nine times out of a hundred, is better than the inside.

HILAIRE BELLOC

At night, when the curtains are drawn and the fire flickers, and the lights are turned off, do my books come into their own, and attain a collective dignity. It is very pleasant to sit with them in the firelight for a couple of minutes, not reading, not even thinking, but aware that they, with their accumulated wisdom and charm, are waiting to be used, and that my library, in its tiny imperfect way, is a successor to the great private libraries of the past.

E. M. FORSTER

The worse for drink, trying to abstract a copy of The Golden Triangle from a glass-fronted bookcase, Bagshaw overturned on himself this massive piece of furniture. As volume after volume descended on him, it was asserted he made the comment: "Books do furnish a room."

ANTHONY POWELL *in A Dance to the Music of Time*

Think what a book is. It is a portion of the eternal mind caught in its process through the world, stamped in an instant, and preserved for eternity.

LORD HOUGHTON

There are books which take rank in our life with parents and lovers and passionate experiences, so medicinal, so stringent, so revolutionary, so authoritative.

RALPH WALDO EMERSON

Each book is a mummified soul embalmed in leather and printer's ink. Each cover of a true book enfolds the concentrated essence of a man. The personalities of the writers have folded into the thinnest shadows, as their bodies into impalpable dust, yet here are their very spirits at your command.

SIR ARTHUR CONAN DOYLE

The true felicity of a lover of books is the luxurious turning of page by page, the surrender, not meanly abject, but deliberate and cautious, with your wits about you, as you deliver yourself into the keeping of the book.

EDITH WHARTON

Mor liked to tear a book apart as he read it, breaking the back, thumbing and turning down the pages, commenting and underlining. He liked to have his books close to him, upon a table, upon the floor, at least upon open shelves. Seeing them so near and so destroyed, he could feel that they were now almost inside his head.

IRIS MURDOCH *(The Sandcastle)*

Books have been my most dependable friends and my unfailing source of pleasure, a mainstay, and the better part of whatever brains I have. It is quite impossible for me to imagine a life without books; not as a substitute for it, but as a continuous and refreshing enrichment.

ASHLEY MONTAGUE

When I see books that I have read on library shelves, it is like running into an old friend on the street. I often take the book down and browse through it, even though I have no intention of checking it out of the library and reading it once again. Like friends, these books have gone into the making of whatever and whoever I am.

KEVIN STARR

The books I read are the ones I knew and loved when I was a young man and to which I return as you do to friends: the Old Testament, Dickens, Conrad, Cervantes — Don Quixote. I read that every year, as some do the Bible. I've read these books so often that I don't always begin at page one and read on to the end. I just read one scene, or about one character just as you'd meet and talk to a friend for a few minutes.

WILLIAM FAULKNER

38

I hold my books up to memory's light, faces gleam, there are whispers from long ago belonging to old friends. I open the books; the characters stretch and pull me back in.

JILL ROBINSON

Most of us who read a lot are abysmally ignorant of books themselves, their fate and history; we cannot tell the difference between a roll and a codex, a chapbook and a plaquette, a colophon and an uncial.

CYRIL CONNOLLY

Of all the inanimate objects, of all of man's creations, books are the nearest to us, for they contain our very thought, our ambitions, our indignations, our illusions, our fidelity to truth, and our persistent leaning towards error. But most of all they resemble us in their precarious hold on life.

JOSEPH CONRAD

Until I see e-books or literary apps that do something that the print book doesn't do better, I'm not very likely to buy into this whole world.

ANDER MONSON

... to yet again take a sheaf of manuscript pages and turn them into something as miraculous and as workable and as permanent as a printed book seems to me worth any amount of trouble.

DAVID R. GODINE, *publisher*

Readers

I so much love to sell books—to match the perfect person with the perfect book. I AM A BOOKSELLER!

MARY SHELDON, *Tecolote Book Shop*

I thank God I am a bookseller, trafficking in the dreams and beauties to curiosities of humanity rather some mere huckster of merchandise.

CHRISTOPHER MORLEY

To put good books in the hands of customers—matchmaking—that's the bookseller's role. If we do it well, we'll stay relevant. If we don't do it well, we won't.

SARAH McNALLY, *McNally Jackson Books*

With the coming of the e-book revolution, it might just be possible that the indies will again become an economic force to be reckoned with, and the idea that bookselling is a vocation, not just a business, will gain new life and a new stature, a virtue to be valued in our hearts.

ANDY ROSS, *Cody's Books*

Don't patronize the chain bookstores. Every time I see some author scheduled to read and sign his books at a chain bookstore, I feel like telling him he's stabbing the independent bookstores in the back.

LAWRENCE FERLINGHETTI

I crave books like I crave chocolate. The need to have a book in my hand overwhelms me. I stalk the aisles searching for the one that speaks to me. Over the course of reading a book, my craving is sated. But it is not long before I begin to crave another.

MEAGHAN BEASELY, *Island Bookstore*

I'm a bookseller, but I'm a feminist bookseller... the real purpose of my life is getting women's voices out, and getting women to tell the truth about their lives.

LINDA BUBON, *Women and Children First Bookstore*

A really good book with a really bad jacket is just really hard to sell. It gives the customer the wrong message.

DANIEL GOLDIN, *Boswell Book Company*

Bookstores offer an experience that is unique. To be able to go into a place physically, to experience a sensation that is the precise opposite of all that is digital, and to talk to people about books. That is, I believe, irreplaceable.

RICHARD HOWORTH, *Square Books*

When I'm walking through the sales floor and a little kid goes up to the shelf and spots a book and says "Oh wow! You've got that book!" To know you've played some small role in making this happen—there's nothing like it.

JOYCE MESKIS, *Tattered Cover Book Store*

Publishers should ask the book to speak first to their own heart. I think that's what readers are asking, and that's what booksellers are asking. They're selling the books that speak deeply to them.

SARAH McNALLY, *McNally Jackson Books*

The bookstore is one of humanity's great engines, one of the greatest instruments of civilization.

CHRISTOPHER MORLEY

To stand in a great bookshop crammed with books so new that their pages almost stick together, and the gilt on their backs is still fresh, has an excitement no less delightful than the old excitement of the second-hand bookstall.

VIRGINIA WOOLF

This bookstore on which bestowed all of my pocket money, was a promised land, fragrant with the crisp aroma of new books and uncut pages—an oasis for a teenager with a newly acquired thirst for literature in a world that had little time for either.

SYLVIE DRAKE

The secondhand stores are hospitable to the seeker of books. They are the only merchandising institutions which encourage the visitor to taste and often consume their wares before making a purchase, or even without making one.

WILLIAM F. McDERMOTT

Some books are to be read in an hour, and returned to the shelf; others require a lifetime to savor their richness. Such books should be owned in personal copies, to travel with and to sleep beside—the most fruitful of all companions. Only your bookseller can consummate such a union of book and reader.

LAWRENCE CLARK POWELL

Booksellers are a race apart and one and all delightful company, as befits those in whom the ideal and the practical are so nicely blended.

CYRIL CONNOLLY

And let us not forget that ineffable, even sensual experience of browsing that will forever be lost in the marketplace of e-books.

ANDY ROSS, *Cody's Books*

A bookstore is one of the only pieces of evidence we have that people are still thinking.

JERRY SEINFELD

A man in a bookstore buys a book on loneliness and every woman in the store hits on him. A woman buys a book on loneliness and the store clears out.

DOUG COUPLAND

I don't browse in bookshops, I browse in libraries, where you can take a book home and read it, and if you like it you go to a bookshop and buy it.

HELENE HANFF

Genre is a bookstore problem, not a literary problem.
RICK MOODY

I can walk into a bookstore and hand over my credit card and they don't know who the hell I am. Maybe that says something about bookstore clerks.
E. L. DOCTOROW

What I say is, a town isn't a town without a bookstore. It may call itself a town, but unless it's got a bookstore it knows it's not fooling a soul.
NEIL GAIMAN

A good bookshop is just a genteel Black Hole that knows how to read.
TERRY PRATCHETT

The smallest bookstore still contains more ideas of worth than have been presented in the entire history of television.
ANDREW ROSS

I get crazy in a bookstore. It makes my heart beat hard because I want to buy everything.
REESE WITHERSPOON

I went to a bookstore and asked the saleswoman, "Where's the self-help section?" She said if she told me, it would defeat the purpose.
GEORGE CARLIN

A book worth reading is worth buying.
JOHN RUSKIN

Book-love, I say again, lasts throughout life, it never flags or fails, but, like Beauty itself, is a joy forever.
HOLBROOK JACKSON

Everyone is in a rush... you don't have the serenity. That, I think, is very important in order to read.
MARIO VARGAS LLOSA

She was not a gentle reader and often wished authors were around so that she could take them to task. It was Henry James she was reading one teatime when she said out loud "Oh, do get *on*."
THE QUEEN *(in Alan Bennett's The Uncommon Reader)*

Sometimes I think heaven must be one continuous unexhausted reading.
VIRGINIA WOOLF

It was always my habit to mark excessively the books I liked. How wonderful it would be, thought I, to see those markings again, to know what were my opinions and reactions in that long ago.
HENRY MILLER

There are books of which the backs and covers are by far the best parts.
CHARLES DICKENS

Genuine poetry can communicate before it is understood.
T.S. ELIOT

Eighty-three percent of American poetry is not worth reading. I haven't done a study, but 83 percent seems like the right number. I think 83 percent of movies aren't worth going to, and 83 percent of restaurants aren't worth eating in. The other 17 percent of poetry isn't just worth reading—I couldn't live without it.
BILLY COLLINS

Books are like Swiss Army knives. They offer endless creative and revealing possibilities for those who like to interact with them.
JOHN MAXWELL HAMILTON

As a former English major, I am a sitting duck for Gift Books, and in the past few years I've gotten Dickens, Thackeray, Smollett, Richardson, Emerson, Keats, Boswell and the Brontës, all of them Great, none of them ever read by me, all of them now on my shelf, looking at me and making me feel guilty.
GARRISON KEILLOR

The books we think we ought to read are poky, dull and dry;
The books that we should like to read we are ashamed to buy;
The books that people talk about we never can recall;
And the books that people give us, oh, they're the worst of all.
CAROLYN WELLS (On Books)

Books are wonderful things: to sit alone in a room and laugh and cry, because you are reading, and still be safe when you close the book; and having finished it, discover you are changed, yet unchanged! To be able to visit the City of Invention at will, depart at will—that is all, really, education is about.

FAY WELDON

It is no accident that books are sacred to civilization. They open the past to us. A book is magical; it transcends time and space.

DANIEL BOORSTIN

My mother read to me in the big bedroom in the mornings, when we were in her rocker together, which ticked in rhythm as we rocked, as though we had a cricket accompanying the story.

EUDORA WELTY

He gave himself up so wholly to the reading of romances that a-nights he would pore on until it was day, and a-days he would read on until it was night; and thus be sleeping little and reading much the moisture of his brain was exhausted to that degree that at last he lost the use of his reason.

MIGUEL DE CERVANTES *(Don Quixote)*

It is not the so-called bad books whose influence I deplore as much as the mediocre ones. The mediocre work, which is the daily fare for most of us, I regard as harmful because it is produced by automatons for automatons. And it is the automatons among us who are more of a hazard to society than the evil ones. If it is our fate to be destroyed by a bomb, it is the sleepwalker who is most apt to do the trick.
HENRY MILLER

If only one person out of a hundred and fifty million should continue as a reader, he would be the one worth saving, the nucleus around which to found a university. This Last Reader might very well stand in the same relation to the community as the queen bee to the colony of bees.... From his nuptial, or intellectual, flight would come the new race of men, linked perfectly with the long past by the unbroken chain of the intellect, to carry on the community.
E. B. WHITE

What about reading in the old, archaic, private, silent sense? This may become as specialized a skill and avocation as it was in the *scriptoria* and libraries of the monasteries during the so-called Dark Ages. The ability, above all, the wish to attend to a demanding text, to master the grammar, the arts of memory, the tactics of repose and concentration which great books demand of us—this may once more become the practice of an elite, of a mandarinate of silence.
GEORGE STEINER

I am never long, even in the society of her I love, without yearning for the company of my lamp and my library.
LORD BYRON

What better occupation, really than to spend the evening at the fireside with a book, with the wind beating on the windows and the lamp burning bright? Without moving, you walk through the countries you see in your mind's eye; and your thoughts, caught up in the story, stop at the details or rush through the plot. You pretend you're the characters and feel it's your own heart beating beneath their costumes.
GUSTAVE FLAUBERT *(Madame Bovary)*

If you can read silently you can read aloud. It takes practice, sure, but it's like playing the guitar: You don't have to be Doc Watson, you can get and give pleasure just pickin'. And a second point: A lot of the stuff we were taught to read silently—Jane! You are moving your lips!—reads better out loud.
URSULA K. LEGUIN

I'll spend the rest of my life reading, and because I'd rather read than do anything else, I don't look forward to years of hopeless, black despair. Most men who are in for life are filled with bitterness and hatred for the unkind fate that led them to such a horrible end.
WILLIE SUTTON, *bank robber*

I never desire to converse with a man who has written more than he has read.
SAMUEL JOHNSON

When you reread a classic, you do not see more in the book than you did before; you see more in you than was there before.

CLIFTON FADIMAN

Just the knowledge that a good book is waiting one at the end of a long day makes that day happier.

KATHLEEN NORRIS

I recite poems to myself all the time as I walk around... I will go on the constitutional required by my doctor and I will just recite poems to myself as I go.

HAROLD BLOOM

To acquire the habit of reading is to construct for yourself a refuge from almost all the miseries of life.

W. SOMERSET MAUGHAM

A good book should leave you slightly exhausted at the end. You live several lives while reading it.

WILLIAM STYRON

Without the enthusiastic reader a book would die. The man who spreads the good word augments not only the life of the book in question but the act of creation itself. He breathes spirit into other readers.

HENRY MILLER

History, real solemn history, I cannot be interested in. The quarrels of popes and kings, with wars or pestilences in every page; the men all so good for nothing, and hardly any women at all.

JANE AUSTEN

Books are like imprisoned souls till someone takes them down from a shelf and frees them.

SAMUEL BUTLER

Coming to the end of some gripping story is like losing a friend. It is no good saying you can read it again. It is never the same the second time.

THE DUCHESS OF DEVONSHIRE

On a nudist beach, I saw a man sitting, naked, entirely engrossed in an issue of *Playboy*. Just like that man, on the inside not on the outside, is where the good reader ought to be while reading.

AMOS OZ

I have always imagined that Paradise will be a kind of library.

JORGE LUIS BORGES

Some books are to be tasted, others to be swallowed, and some few to be chewed and digested.

FRANCIS BACON

Books are to be called for and supplied on the assumption that the process of reading is not a half sleep but in the highest sense an exercise, a gymnastic struggle; that the reader is to do something for himself.

WALT WHITMAN

Not for nothing were slaves in South Carolina threatened with the loss of the first joint of their forefingers if they were caught looking at a book. The truth shall make you free.

ANNE QUINDLEN

A book should serve as the axe for the frozen sea within us.

FRANZ KAFKA

You can teach a child to read, and he or her will be able to pass a literacy test.

GEORGE W. BUSH

Whenever you read a good book, it's like the author is right there, in the room talking to you, which is why I don't like to read good books.

JACK HANDY

Everyone probably thinks that I'm a raving nymphomaniac, that I have an insatiable sexual appetite, when the truth is I'd rather read a book.

MADONNA

....

And I read until my fingers were raw, and there were words racing through my head and I didn't have to talk or ask too many questions. I loved the quiet in the house when my parents were sleeping when I was alone with my hands.
MARY McGINNIS, *from her Reading Braille*

There is a wonder in reading Braille that the sighted will never know: to touch words and have them touch you back.
JIM FIEBIG

Until I feared I would lose it, I never loved to read. One does not love breathing.
HARPER LEE

If the book is good, is about something that you know, and is truly written, and reading it over you see that this is so, you can let the boys yip and the noise will have that pleasant sound coyotes make on a very cold night when they are out in the snow and you are in your own cabin that you have built or paid for with your work.
ERNEST HEMINGWAY

Reading isn't good for a ballplayer. Not good for his eyes. If my eyes went bad even a little bit I couldn't hit home runs. So I gave up reading.
BABE RUTH

No two persons ever read the same book.
EDMUND WILSON

The greatest gift is a passion for reading. It is cheap, it consoles, it distracts, it excites, it gives you knowledge of the world and experience of a wide kind. It is a moral illumination.

ELIZABETH HARDWICK

Almost nothing in our culture encourages the private moment of reading.

ELIZABETH SIFTON

I find it the hardest thing in the world to read almost any new novel. Any is hard enough, but the hardest from the innocent hands of young females perhaps above all.

HENRY JAMES *(the book was The Troll Garden by Willa Cather)*

I bought a book by Henry James yesterday and read it, as they say, "until far into the night". It was not very interesting or very good, but I can wade through pages and pages of dull, turgid James for the sake of that sudden, sweet shock, that violent throb of delight that he gives me at times.

KATHERINE MANSFIELD

When or where I learned to read, I could never remember. When I look back, it seems to me that one day the alphabet was merely a row of black or white marks on paper, and the next day I was earnestly picking out the letters in *Old Mortality*.

ELLEN GLASGOW

The more I like a book, the more slowly I read. This spontaneous talking back to a book is one of the things that makes reading so valuable.

ANATOLE BROYARD

Reading, after a certain age, diverts the mind too much from its creative pursuits. Any man who reads too much and uses his own brain too little falls into lazy habits of thinking.

ALBERT EINSTEIN

There are few things I enjoy so much as talking to people about books which I have read and they haven't, and making them wish they had—preferably a book that is hard to get or in a language that they do not know.

EDMUND WILSON

I would sooner read a timetable or a catalog than nothing at all.

W. SOMERSET MAUGHAM

The discovery I made was that any number of stories are really meant to work, and only work, in the mind's ear and hearing them out loud diminishes their effectiveness. Some of course hold up amusingly, but it's no fun hearing a story that's really meant to be read. It's hard to beat sitting in bed or in a comfortable chair turning the pages of a book, putting it down, and eagerly awaiting the chance to get back to it.

WOODY ALLEN, *on reading versus an audio book*

If you read a lot of books you are considered well read. But if you watch a lot of TV, you're not considered well viewed.

LILY TOMLIN

When I was your age, television was called books. And this is a special book. It was the book my father used to read to me when I was sick, and I used to read it to your father. And today I'm gonna read it to you.

PETER FALK, *as Grandpa in The Princess Bride*

In my teens I spent a lot of time at the new public library. My aunt patronized the private lending library at Boots the Chemist. But growing curious about my library, she followed me there and was dazzled by what she saw and, like many middle-class people round the country, became a convert to the public library system. Being cautious, she would lightly toast the books in our oven for the sake of the germs.

MICHAEL HOLROYD

I write for the girl I once was, who found paradise in the pages of a book and pure music in the characters' voices, which were strong enough to drown the summer-long drone of Phil Rizzuto calling out line drives to left field on my father's ancient, crackling table radio.

RITA CIRESI

I grew up around a father and mother who read every chance they got, who took us to the library every Thursday night to load up on books for the coming week. Most nights after dinner my father stretched out on the couch to read, while my mother sat with her book in the easy chair and the three of us kids each retired to our own private reading stations.

ANNE LAMOTT

I knew a gentleman who was so good a manager of his time that he would not even lose that small portion of it which the calls of nature obliged him to pass in the necessary-house; but gradually went through all the Latin poets in those moments.

LORD CHESTERFIELD

Reading—the best state yet to keep absolute loneliness at bay.

WILLIAM STYRON

"Tell me what you read and I'll tell you who you are" is true enough, but I'd know you better if you told me what you reread.

FRANCOIS MAURIAC

If one cannot enjoy reading a book over and over again, there is no use in reading it at all.

OSCAR WILDE

The more that you read,
the more things you will know.
The more that you learn,
the more places you'll go.
DR. SEUSS

Reading a poem in January is as lovely as to go for a walk in June.
JEAN PAUL

Reading is like the sex act—done privately, and often in bed.
DANIEL BOORSTIN

Software is usually accompanied by documentation in the form of big fat scary manuals that nobody ever reads. In fact, for the past five years most of the manuals shipped with software products have actually been copies of Stephen King's *The Stand* with new covers pasted on.
DAVE BARRY

There are some books of which scores of copies are bought for one which is read, and others which have dozens of readers for every copy sold.
JOHN AYSCOUGH

What a sense of superiority it gives one to escape reading a book which everyone else is reading.
ALICE JAMES

Some writers thrive with the contact with the commerce of success; others are corrupted by it. Perhaps, like losing one's virginity it is not as bad (or as good) as one feared it was going to be.

V.S. PRITCHETT

When I am dead, I hope it may be said:
"His sins were scarlet, but his books were read."

HILAIRE BELLOC

There are two motives for reading a book; one, that you enjoy it; the other, that you can boast about it.

BERTRAND RUSSELL

A "bestseller" is a celebrity among books. It is known primarily (sometimes exclusively) for its well-knownness.

DANIEL BOORSTIN

There are books and there is literature. I have never met anyone who bought a book on the bestseller lists.

ELIZABETH HARDWICK

A bestseller is the gilded tomb of a mediocre talent.

LOGAN PEARSALL SMITH

There are some books one needs maturity to enjoy just as there are books an adult can come upon too late to savor.

PHYLLIS McGINLEY

No book is really worth reading at the age of ten which is not equally (and often far more) worth reading at the age of fifty and beyond.

C.S. LEWIS

The stories of childhood leave an indelible impression, and their author always has a niche in the temple of memory from which the image is never cast out to be thrown on the rubbish heap of things that are outgrown and outlived.

HOWARD PYLE

The road to ignorance is paved with good editions.

GEORGE BERNARD SHAW

Every man who knows how to read has it in his power to magnify himself, to multiply the ways in which he exists, to make his life full, significant and interesting.

ALDOUS HUXLEY

When we read too fast or too slowly we understand nothing.

BLAISE PASCAL

Who knows if Shakespeare might not have thought less if he had read more.

EDWARD YOUNG

The oldest books are still only just out to those who have not read them.

SAMUEL BUTLER

Reading is to the mind what exercise is to the body.
SIR RICHARD STEELE

The best effect of any book is that it excites the reader to self-activity.
THOMAS CARLYLE

A man may as well expect to grow stronger by always eating as wiser by always reading.
JEREMY COLLIER

I would never read a book if it were possible for me to talk half an hour with the man who wrote it.
WOODROW WILSON

No woman was ever ruined by a book.
MAYOR JIMMY WALKER *of New York City*

Those whom books will hurt will not be proof against events. If some books are deemed more baneful and their sale forbid, how, then, with deadlier facts, not dreams of doting men? Events, not books, should be forbid.
HERMAN MELVILLE

There is a great deal of difference between an eager man who wants to read a book and a tired man who wants a book to read.
G.K. CHESTERTON

I divide all readers into two classes; those who read to remember and those who read to forget.

WILLIAM LYON PHELPS

As a rule reading fiction is as hard to me as trying to hit a target by hurling feathers at it. I need resistance to cerebrate!

WILLIAM JAMES

A book is a mirror; if an ass peers into it, you can't expect an apostle to peer out.

GEORG CHRISTOPH LICHTENBERG

When you reread a classic you do not see more in the book than you did before; you see more in *you* than was there before.

CLIFTON FADIMAN

The art of reading is in great part that of acquiring a better understanding of life from one's encounter with it in a book.

ANDRE MAUROIS

I suggest that the only books that influence us are those for which we are ready, and which have gone a little farther down our particular path than we have yet gone ourselves.

E.M. FORSTER

Only one hour in the normal day is more pleasurable than the hour spent in bed with a book before going to sleep, and that is the hour spent in bed with a book after being called in the morning.

ROSE MACAULAY

The pleasure of all reading is doubled when one lives with another who shares the same books.

KATHERINE MANSFIELD

I can't wait to run against a President who owns more tuxedos than books.

SENATOR GARY HART

In a very real sense, people who have read good literature have lived more than people who cannot or will not read. It is not true that we have only one life to live; if we can read, we can live as many more lives and as many kinds of lives as we wish.

S.I. HAYAKAWA

It is absurd to have a hard-and-fast rule about what one should read and what one shouldn't. More than half of modern culture depends on what one shouldn't read.

OSCAR WILDE

There are times when I think that the reading I have done in the past has had no effect except to cloud my mind and make me indecisive.

ROBERTSON DAVIES

If I read a book that impresses me, I have to take myself firmly in hand before I mix with other people; otherwise they would think my mind rather queer.

ANNE FRANK

There is more treasure in books than in all the pirates' loot on Treasure Island, and best of all, you can enjoy these riches every day of your life.

WALT DISNEY

Bookful blockhead, ignorantly read,
With loads of learned lumber in his head.

ALEXANDER POPE

A reader finds little in a book save what he puts there. But in a great book he finds space to put many things.

JOSEPH JOUBERT

Lay down a method also for your reading; let it be in a consistent and consecutive course, and not in that desultory and unmethodical manner, in which many people read scraps of different authors, upon different subjects.

EARL OF CHESTERFIELD

There are only four kinds of readers. The first is like the hour-glass; their reading being as the sand, it runs in and runs out, and leaves no vestige behind. The second is like the sponge, which imbibes everything, and returns it in nearly the same state, only a little dirtier. A third is like a jelly-bag, allowing all that is pure to pass away, retaining only the refuse and dregs. And the fourth is like the slaves in the diamond mines, who, casting aside all that is worthless, retain only pure gems.

SAMUEL TAYLOR COLERIDGE

The profit of books is according to the sensibility of the reader. The profoundest thought or passion sleeps as in a mine, until an equal mind finds and publishes it.

RALPH WALDO EMERSON

To read a book in the truest sense, to read it, that is, not as a critic but in the spirit of enjoyment—is to lay aside for the moment one's own personality and to become a part of the author.

LESLIE STEPHEN

A good reader is one who has imagination, memory, a dictionary, and some artistic sense.

VLADIMIR NABOKOV

If anyone finds that he never reads serious literature, if all his reading is frothy and trashy, he would do well to try to train himself to like books that the general agreement of cultivated and sound-thinking persons has placed among the classics. It is as discreditable to the mind to be unfit for sustained mental effort as it is to the body of a young man to be unfit for sustained physical effort.

THEODORE ROOSEVELT

In anything fit to be called by the name of reading, the process itself should be absorbing and voluptuous; we should gloat over a book, be rapt clean out of ourselves.

ROBERT LOUIS STEVENSON

No book, any more than helpful words, can do anything decisive if the person concerned is not already prepared through quite invisible influences for a deeper receptivity and absorption, if his hour of self-communion has not come anyway.

RAINER MARIA RILKE

The adult relation to books is one of absorbing rather than being absorbed.

ANTHONY BURGESS

One only reads well that which one reads with some quite personal purpose. It may be to acquire some power. It can be out of hatred for the author.

PAUL VALERY

There is only one situation I can think of in which men and women make an effort to read better than they usually do. When they are in love and reading a love letter, they read for all they are worth.

MORTIMER J. ADLER

If the book we are reading does not wake us, as with a fist hammering on our skull, why then do we read it? But what we must have are those books which come upon us like ill-fortune, and distress us deeply, like the death of one we love better than ourselves, like suicide.

FRANZ KAFKA

To read great literature as if it did not have upon us an urgent design is to do little more than to make entries in a librarian's catalogue.

GEORGE STEINER

To read a book, in my own case, is always a sort of combat, in which I ask myself whether the author is going to overcome me, and persuade me, and convince me, or even vex me.

ARTHUR CHRISTOPHER BENSON

As you read a book word by word and page by page, you participate in its creation, just as a cellist playing a Bach suite participates, note by note, in the creation, the coming-to-be, the existence, of the music. And, as you read and re-read, the book of course participates in the creation of *you*, your thoughts and feelings, the size and temper of your soul.

URSULA K. LEGUIN

The process of reading is reciprocal: the book is no more than a formula, to be furnished out with images out of the reader's mind.

ELIZABETH BOWEN

In reality every reader is, while he is reading, the reader of his own self.

MARCEL PROUST

The novelist in America today benefits from a group of readers who, beset with an unprecedented variety of diversions, continue to read with great taste and intelligence.

JOHN CHEEVER

Unless a reader is able to give something of himself, he cannot get from a novel the best it has to give. And if he isn't able to do that, he had better not read it at all. There is no obligation to read a work of fiction.

W. SOMERSET MAUGHAM

A book consists of two layers: on top, the readable layer and underneath, a layer that was inaccessible. You only sense its existence in a moment of distraction from the literal reading, the way you see childhood through a child. It would take forever to tell what you see, and it would be pointless.

MARGUERITE DURAS

It's not macho to read a book? Nonsense. Reading is a stouthearted activity, disporting courage, keenness, stick-to-it-ness. It is also, in my experience, one of the most thrilling and enduring delights of life, equal to a home run, a slam-dunk, or breaking the four-minute mile.

IRVING STONE

Reading at its most demanding is, purely and simply, hard, which is precisely why we are so eager to be done with it.

JONATHAN YARDLEY

I claim that this bookless library is a dream, a hallucination of on-line addicts; network neophytes, and library-automation insiders... Instead, I suspect computers will deviously chew away at libraries from the inside. They'll eat up book budgets and require librarians that are more comfortable with computers than with children and scholars. Libraries will become adept at supplying the public with fast, low-quality information.

The result won't be a library without books—it'll be a library without value.

CLIFFORD STOLL

There are quite a number of people in the reading room; but one is not aware of them. They are inside the books. They move, sometimes, within the pages like sleepers turning over between two dreams. Ah, how good it is to be among people who are reading!

RAINER MARIA RILKE

The library profession is informed, illuminated, radiated, by a fierce and beautiful love of books. A love so overwhelming that it engulfs community after community and makes the culture of our time distinctive, individual, creative and truly of the spirit.

FRANCES CLARKE SAYERS

People can lose their lives in libraries. They ought to be warned.

SAUL BELLOW

Befiehl dem Herrn deine Wege
u. hoffe auf ihn er wirds wohl
machen.

In a library we are surrounded by many hundreds of dear friends imprisoned by an enchanter in paper and leathern boxes.
RALPH WALDO EMERSON

The library smells, a combination of Lily of the Valley cologne, damp wells, library paste and wet wool snowsuits, were as distinctive as the smell of my childhood home.
JUDITH ST. GEORGE

The uniqueness of the library is the joy of discovery. You find material that you were never looking for.
ANNETTE MACNAIR

No university in the world has ever risen to greatness without a great library, and no university is greater than its library.
VARTAN GREGORIAN

There is one type of building which is profane yet in fulfilling its proper role touches the hem of the sacred: the great library.
SIR COLIN ST. JOHN WILSON

May this structure throned on imperishable books be maintained and cherished from generation to generation for the improvement and delight of mankind.
Inscription at Old Main Library, San Francisco

The library—my refuge, my shelter, my source, resource, joy—where I browsed hungrily through the stacks, finding my teacher, my inspiration, my companions.
TILLIE OLSEN

A great library cannot be constructed—it is the growth of ages.
JOHN HILL BURTON

What a place to be is an old library! It seems as though all the souls of all the writers, that have bequested their labours were reposing here.
CHARLES LAMB

When I was a boy in Pittsburgh, Colonel Anderson of Allegheny—a name I can never speak without feelings of devotional gratitude—opened his little library of four hundred books to boys every Saturday afternoon. He was in attendance himself. No one but he who has felt it can know the intense longing with which the arrival of Saturday was awaited.
ANDREW CARNEGIE

I read library books as fast as I could go, rushing them home in the basket of my bicycle. From the minute I reached our house, I started to read. The only fear was that of books coming to an cnd.
EUDORA WELTY

Whenever I was free to read, the great library seemed free to receive me. Anything I had heard of and wanted to see the blessed place owned.
ALFRED KAZIN, *on the New York Public Library*

It is necessary to have £500 a year and a room with a lock on the door if you are to write fiction or poetry.
VIRGINIA WOOLF

Everyone who works in the domain of fiction is a bit crazy. The problem is to render this craziness interesting.
FRANCOIS TRUFFAUT

There's many a best-seller that could have been prevented by a good writing teacher. The idea of being a writer attracts a good many shiftless people, those who are burdened by poetic feelings or afflicted with sensibility.
FLANNERY O'CONNOR

The greatest masterpiece in literature is only a dictionary out of order.
JEAN COCTEAU

You don't put your life into your books. You find it there.
THE QUEEN *(in Alan Bennett's The Uncommon Reader)*

Language is the soul's ozone layer and we thin it at our peril.
SVEN BIRKERTS

Read, read, read. Read everything—trash, classics, good and bad, and see how they do it. Just like a carpenter who works as an apprentice and studies the master. Read! You'll absorb it. Then write. If it is good, you'll find out. If it's not, throw it out the window.
WILLIAM FAULKNER

Literature is an occupation in which you have to keep proving your talent to people who have none.

JULES RENARD

One of the most common and saddest spectacles is that of a person of really fine sensibility and acute psychological perception trying to write fiction by using these qualities alone. This type of writer will put down one intensely emotional or keenly perceptive sentence after the other, and the result will be complete dullness. The fact is that the materials of the fiction writer are the humblest. Fiction is about everything human and we are made out of dust, and if you scorn getting yourself dusty, then you shouldn't try to write fiction. It's not a grand enough job for you.

FLANNERY O'CONNOR

The impulse to keep to yourself what you have learned is not only shameful, it is destructive. Anything you do not give freely and abundantly becomes lost to you. You open your safe and find ashes.

ANNIE DILLARD

Pursue, keep up with, circle round and round your life... know your own bone; gnaw at it, bury it, unearth it, and gnaw at it still.

H.D. THOREAU

The last thing that we find in making a book is to know what we must put first.

BLAISE PASCAL

Literature was not born the day when a boy crying "wolf, wolf "came running out of the Neanderthal valley with a big gray wolf at this heels: literature was born on the day when a boy came crying "wolf, wolf" and there was no wolf behind him.

VLADIMIR NABOKOV

The players often mention it as an honor to Shakespeare that in his writing, whatsoever he penned, he never blotted out a line. My answer hath been, "Would he had blotted a thousand."

BEN JONSON

I have not wasted my life trifling with literary fools in taverns as Jonson did when he should have been shaking England with the thunder of his spirit.

GEORGE BERNARD SHAW

Of course no writers ever forget their first acceptance. One fine day when I was seventeen I had my first, second and third, all in the same morning's mail. Oh, I'm here to tell you, dizzy with excitement is no mere phrase!

TRUMAN CAPOTE

Publication—is the auction of the Mind of Man.

EMILY DICKINSON

If there is a special Hell for writers it would be in the forced contemplation of their own works, with all the misconceptions, the omissions, the failures that any finished work of art implies.

JOHN DOS PASSOS

On the day when a young writer corrects his first proof-sheet he is as proud as a schoolboy who has just gotten his first dose of the pox.

CHARLES BAUDELAIRE

Most of the basic material a writer works with is acquired before the age of fifteen.

WILLA CATHER

However great a man's natural talent may be, the art of writing cannot be learned all at once.

JEAN JACQUES ROUSSEAU

When I was twenty I was in love with words, a wordsmith. I didn't know enough to know when people were letting words get in their way. Now I like the words to disappear, like a transparent curtain.

WALLACE STEGNER

I have never been good at revising. I always thought I made things worse by recasting and retouching. I never knew what was meant by choice of words. It was one word or none.

ROBERT FROST

As for my next book, I am going to hold myself from writing it till I have it impending in me: grown heavy in my mind like a ripe pear; pendant, gravid, asking to be cut or it will fall.

VIRGINIA WOOLF

When I read my first book, I started writing my first book. I have never not been writing.

GORE VIDAL

Looking back, I imagine I was always writing. Twaddle it was too. But better far write twaddle or anything, anything, than nothing at all.

KATHERINE MANSFIELD

I suppose I am a born novelist, for the things I imagine are more vital and vivid to me than the things I remember.

ELLEN GLASGOW

If we should ever inaugurate a hall of fame, it would be reserved exclusively and hopefully for authors who, having written four bestsellers, still refrained from starting out on a lecture tour.

E.B WHITE

A good title should be like a good metaphor: It should intrigue without being too baffling or too obvious.

WALKER PERCY

Almost anyone can be an author; the business is to collect money and fame from this state of being.

A.A. MILNE

Writing is the only profession where no one considers you ridiculous if you earn no money.

JULES RENARD

Sir, no man but a blockhead ever wrote except for money.

SAMUEL JOHNSON

The profession of book-writing makes horse racing seem like a solid, stable business.

JOHN STEINBECK

If writers were good businessmen, they'd have too much sense to be writers.

IRVIN S. COBB

The multitude of books is a great evil. There is no measure or limit to this fever of writing; everyone must be an author, some for some kind of vanity to acquire celebrity and raise a name, others for the sake of lucre or gain.

MARTIN LUTHER

I do think that the quality which makes a man want to write and be read is essentially a desire for self-exposure and is masochistic. Like one of those guys who has a compulsion to take his thing out and show it on the street.

JAMES JONES

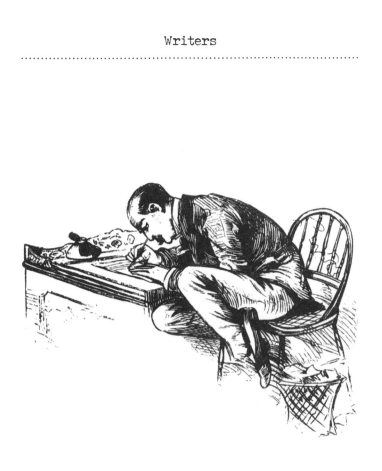

Almost all the great writers have as their motif, more or less disguised, the "passage from childhood to maturity," the clash between the thrill of expectation, and the disillusioning knowledge of the truth. Lost Illusion is the undisclosed title of every novel.

ANDRE MAUROIS

I'm terrible about titles; I don't know how to come up with them. They're the one thing in the story I'm really uncertain about.

EUDORA WELTY

Sometimes people give titles to me, and sometimes I see them on a billboard.

ROBERT PENN WARREN

I don't want to take up literature in a money-making spirit, or be very anxious about making large profits, but selling it at a loss is another thing altogether, and an amusement I cannot well afford.

LEWIS CARROLL

Instead of marvelling with Johnson, how anything but profit should incite men to literary labour, I am rather surprised that mere emolument should induce them to labour so well.

THOMAS GREEN

One of the least impressive liberties is the liberty to starve. This particular liberty is freely accorded to authors.

LORD GOODMAN

Years ago, to say you were a writer was not the highest recommendation to your landlord. Today, he at least hesitates before he refuses to rent you an apartment—for all he knows you may be rich.

ARTHUR MILLER

When one says that a writer is fashionable one practically always means that he is admired by people under thirty.

GEORGE ORWELL

The secret of popular writing is never to put more on a given page than the common reader can lap off it with no strain whatsoever on his habitually slack attention.

EZRA POUND

An author is a person who can never take innocent pleasure in visiting a bookstore again. Say you go in and discover that there are no copies of your book on the shelves. You resent all the other books—I don't care if they are Great Expectations, Life on the Mississippi, and the King James Bible—that are on the shelves.

ROY BLOUNT, JR.

A man really writes for an audience of about ten persons. Of course, if others like it, that is clear gain. But if those ten are satisfied, he is content.

ALFRED NORTH WHITEHEAD

I write what I would like to read—what I think other women would like to read. If what I write makes a woman in the Canadian mountains cry and she writes and tells me about it, especially if she says "I read it to Tom when he came in from work and he cried too," I feel I have succeeded.

> KATHLEEN NORRIS, *on the publication of her seventy-eighth book*

When I was a ten-year-old book worm and used to kiss the dust jacket pictures of authors as if they were icons, it used to amaze me that these remote people could provoke me to love.

> ERICA JONG

Anything that is written to please the author is worthless.

> BLAISE PASCAL

I'm a lousy writer; a helluva lot of people have got lousy taste.

> GRACE METALIOUS

Those big-shot writers... could never dig the fact that there are more salted peanuts consumed than caviar.

> MICKEY SPILLANE

I try to leave out the parts that people skip.

> ELMORE LEONARD

Any writer overwhelmingly honest about pleasing himself is almost sure to please others.

> MARIANNE MOORE

My purpose is to entertain myself first and other people secondly.

JOHN D. MACDONALD

When I write, I aim in my mind not toward New York but toward a vague spot a little east of Kansas. I think of the books on library shelves, without their jackets, years old, and a countryish teen-aged boy finding them, and having them speak to him. The reviews, the stacks in Brentano's, are just hurdles to get over, to place the books on that shelf.

JOHN UPDIKE

A kid is a guy I never wrote down to. He's interested in what I say if I make it interesting. He is also the last container of a sense of humor, which disappears as he gets older, and he laughs only according to the way the boss, society, politics, or race want him to. Then he becomes an adult. And an adult is an obsolete child.

DR. SEUSS

The public and the reviewers have always given way, and always give way, to the idiosyncrasies of an author who is strong enough to make them. The history of literature is nothing but the performance of authors of feats which the best experience had declared could not be performed.

ARNOLD BENNETT

I do not believe the expenditure of $2.50 for a book entitles the purchaser to the personal friendship of the author.

EVELYN WAUGH

Having your book turned into a movie is like seeing your oxen turned into bouillon cubes.

JOHN LECARRÉ

Writers, if they are worthy of that jealous designation, do not write for other writers. They write to give reality to experience.

ARCHIBALD MACLEISH

A man who writes well writes not as others write, but as he himself writes; it is often in speaking badly that he speaks well.

MONTESQUIEU

In a very real sense, the writer writes in order to teach himself, to understand himself, to satisfy himself; the publishing of his ideas, though it brings gratifications, is a curious anticlimax.

ALFRED KAZIN

Success comes to a writer, as a rule, so gradually that it is always something of a shock to him to look back and realize the heights to which he has climbed.

P.G. WODEHOUSE

America is about the last place in which life will be endurable at all for an inspired writer.

SAMUEL BUTLER

In America only the successful writer is important, in France all writers are important, in England no writer is important, in Australia you have to explain what a writer is.

GEOFFREY COTTERELL

A Frenchman can humiliate an Englishman just as readily as an Englishman can humiliate an American, and an American a Canadian. One of Canada's most serious literary needs is some lesser nation to domineer over and shame by displays of superior taste.

ROBERTSON DAVIES

Literature plays an important role in our country, helping the Party to educate the people correctly, to instill in them advanced, progressive ideas by which our Party is guided. And it is not without reason that writers in our country are called engineers of the human soul.

NIKITA KHRUSHCHEV

No wonder the really powerful men in our society, whether politicians or scientists, hold writers and poets in contempt. They do it because they get no evidence from modern literature that anybody is thinking about any significant question.

SAUL BELLOW

To write is to write is to write is to write is to write is to write is to write is to write.

GERTRUDE STEIN

Word has somehow got around that the split infinitive is always wrong. That is a piece with the outworn notion that it is always wrong to strike a lady.

JAMES THURBER

The difference between the right word and the nearly right word is the same as that between lightning and the lightning bug.

MARK TWAIN

You can be a little ungrammatical if you come from the right part of the country.

ROBERT FROST

I often think how much easier life would have been for me and how much time I would have saved if I had known the alphabet. I can never tell where I and J stand without saying G, H to myself first. I don't know whether P comes before R or after, and where T comes in has to this day remained something that I have never been able to get into my head.

W. SOMERSET MAUGHAM

Any writer worth the name is always getting into one thing or getting out of another thing.

FANNIE HURST

At its best our age is an age of searchers, and at its worst, an age that has domesticated despair and learned to live with it happily. The fiction which celebrates this last state will be the least likely to transcend its limitations, for when the religious need is banished successfully, it usually atrophies, even in the novelist. The sense of mystery vanishes. A kind of reverse evolution takes place, and the whole range of feeling is dulled.

FLANNERY O'CONNOR

In conversation you can use timing, a look, inflection, pauses. But on the page all you have is commas, dashes, the amount of syllables in a word. When I write I read everything out loud to get the right rhythm.

FRAN LEBOWITZ

Writing is easy; all you do is sit staring at a blank sheet of paper until the drops of blood form on your forehead.

GENE FOWLER

When I hear about writer's block, this one and that one! f**k off! Stop writing, for Christ's sake: Plenty more where you came from.

GORE VIDAL

I lost everything at Philippi, and took to poetry to make a living, but now I have a competence I should be mad if I did not prefer ease to writing.

HORACE

When I stepped from hard manual work to writing, I just stepped from one kind of hard work to another.

SEAN O'CASEY

Nothing you write, if you hope to be any good, will ever come out as you first hoped.

LILLIAN HELLMAN

I can't write five words but that I change seven.

DOROTHY PARKER

If you are getting the worst of it in an argument with a literary man, always attack his style. That'll touch him if nothing else will.

J.A. SPENDER

In stating as fully as I could how things really were, it was often very difficult and I wrote awkwardly and the awkwardness is what they called my style. All mistakes and awkwardness are easy to see, and they called it style.

ERNEST HEMINGWAY

I have written—often several times—every word I have every published. My pencils outlast their erasures.

VLADIMIR NABOKOV

I quit writing if I feel inspired, because I know I'm going to have to throw it away. Writing a novel is like building a wall brick by brick; only amateurs believe in inspiration.

FRANK YERBY

... there are days when the result is so bad that no fewer than five revisions are required. In contrast, when I'm greatly inspired, only four revisions are needed.

JOHN KENNETH GALBRAITH

You will have to write and put away or burn a lot of material before you are comfortable in this medium. You might as well start now and get the necessary work done. For I believe that eventually quantity will make for quality.

RAY BRADBURY

I write a lot—every day, seven days a week—and I throw a lot away. Sometimes I think I write to throw away; it's a process of distillation.

DONALD BARTHELME

The wastepaper basket is the writer's best friend.

ISAAC B. SINGER

Read over your compositions and when you meet a passage which you think is particularly fine, strike it out.

SAMUEL JOHNSON

To write simply is as difficult as to be good.

W. SOMERSET MAUGHAM

A bad book is as much a labor to write as a good one; it comes as sincerely from the author's soul.

ALDOUS HUXLEY

It takes less time to learn to write nobly than to learn to write lightly and straightforwardly.

FRIEDRICH NIETZSCHE

All a writer has to do is get a woman to say he's a writer; it's an aphrodisiac.

SAUL BELLOW

Pretty women swarm around everybody but writers. Plain, intelligent women somewhat swarm around writers.

WILLIAM SAROYAN

If you were a member of Jesse James' band and people asked you what you were, you wouldn't say, "Well, I'm a desperado." You'd say something like "I work in banks" or "I've done some railroad work." It took me a long time just to say "I'm a writer." It's really embarrassing.

ROY BLOUNT, JR.

Most writers are in a state of gloom a good deal of the time; they need perpetual reassurance.

JOHN HALL WHEELOCK

It's my experience that very few writers, young or old, are really seeking advice when they give out their work to be read. They want support; they want someone to say, "Good job".

JOHN IRVING

Writing is not a profession but a vocation of unhappiness.

GEORGES SIMENON

Writing a book is not as tough as it is to haul 35 people around the country and sweat like a horse five nights a week.
BETTE MIDLER

For forty-odd years in this noble profession
I've harbored a guilt and my conscience is smitten.
So here is my slightly embarrassed confession—
I don't like to write, but I love to have written.
MICHAEL KANIN

I love being a writer. What I can't stand is the paperwork.
PETER DE VRIES

It is a fact that few novelists enjoy the creative labour, though most enjoy thinking about the creative labour.
ARNOLD BENNETT

What release to write so that one forgets oneself, forgets one's companion, forgets where one is or what one is going to do next—to be drenched in sleep or in the sea. Pencils and pads and curling blue sheets alive with letters heap up on the desk.
ANNE MORROW LINDBERGH

I am convinced that all writers are optimists whether they concede the point or not. How otherwise could any human being sit down to a pile of blank sheets and decide to write, say two hundred thousand words on a given theme?
THOMAS COSTAIN

....

If we had to say what writing is, we would define it essentially as an act of courage.

    CYNTHIA OZICK

Whatever our theme in writing, it is old and tried. Whatever our place, it has been visited by the stranger, it will never be new again. It is only the vision that can be new; but that is enough.

    EUDORA WELTY

Every good story is a parable.

    FLANNERY O'CONNOR

The writer, like the priest, must be exempted from secular labor. His work needs a frolic health; he must be at the top of his condition.

    RALPH WALDO EMERSON

The writer has taken unto himself the former function of the priest or prophet. He presumes to order and legislate the people's life. There is no person more arrogant than the writer.

    CORNELIUS REGISTER

It took me fifteen years to discover I had no talent for writing, but I couldn't give it up because by that time I was too famous.

    ROBERT BENCHLEY

You must not suppose, because I am a man of letters, that I never tried to earn an honest living.

> GEORGE BERNARD SHAW

An incurable itch for scribbling takes possession of many and grows inveterate in their insane hearts.

> JUVENAL

Another damned thick, square book! Always scribble, scribble! Eh! Mr. Gibbon?

> THE DUKE OF GLOUCESTER, *upon accepting the second volume of A History of the Decline and Fall of the Roman Empire from its author*

The devoted writer of humor must continue to try to come as close to the truth as he can, even if he gets burned in the process, but I don't think he will get too badly burned. His faith in the good will, the soundness, and the sense of humor of his countrymen will always serve as his asbestos curtain.

> JAMES THURBER

It's much easier to write a solemn book than a funny book. It's harder to make people laugh than it is to make them cry. People are always on the verge of tears.

> FRAN LEBOWITZ

Boozing does not necessarily have to go hand in hand with being a writer, as seems to be the concept in America. I therefore solemnly declare to all young men trying to become writers that they do not actually have to become drunkards first.

NELSON ALDRICH

Some American writers who have known each other for years have never met in the daytime or when both were sober.

JAMES THURBER

I put a piece of paper under my pillow, and when I could not sleep I wrote in the dark.

H. D. THOREAU

I put things down on sheets of paper and stuff them in my pockets. When I have enough, I have a book.

JOHN LENNON

Failure is very difficult for a writer to bear, but very few can manage the shock of early success.

MAURICE VALENCY

This is what I find encouraging about the writing trades: They allow mediocre people who are patient and industrious to revise their stupidity, to edit themselves into something like intelligence. They also allow lunatics to seem saner than sane.

KURT VONNEGUT, JR.

From the moment I picked your book up until I laid it down I was convulsed with laughter. Someday I intend reading it.

GROUCHO MARX, *on S.J. Perelman's first book*

It is the part of prudence to thank an author for his book before reading it, so as to avoid the necessity of lying about it afterwards.

GEORGE SANTAYANA

No one can write decently who is distrustful of the reader's intelligence, or whose attitude is patronizing.

E.B. WHITE

They always think that if you write well you're somehow cheating, you're not being democratic by writing as badly as everybody else does.

GORE VIDAL

If you want to get rich from writing, write the sort of thing that's read by persons who move their lips when they're reading to themselves.

DON MARQUIS

In my opinion the readers of novels are far more intelligent than unsuccessful writers will believe. They are expert in detecting and merciless to the conceited author, and the insincere author, and the author with all the tools of literature at his command who has nothing to say worth reading.

NEVIL SHUTE

. GOLD AND SILVER PENCILS. (Hall Marked.)

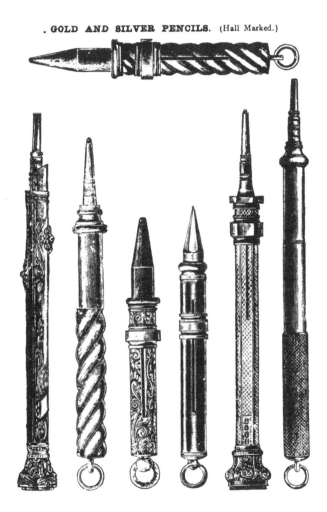

Everything goes by the board: honor, pride, decency... to get the book written. If a writer has to rob his mother, he will not hesitate; the Ode on a Grecian Urn is worth any number of old ladies.

WILLIAM FAULKNER

The most essential gift for a good writer is a built-in shock-proof shit-detector.

ERNEST HEMINGWAY

Nature, not content with denying him the ability to think, has endowed him with the ability to write.

A.E. HOUSMAN

Writing is an adventure. To begin with, it is a toy and an amusement. Then it becomes a mistress, then it becomes a master, then it becomes a tyrant. The last phase is that just as you are about to be reconciled to your servitude, you kill the monster and fling him to the public.

WINSTON CHURCHILL

In literature today, there are plenty of masons but few good architects.

JOSEPH JOUBERT

The difference between journalism and literature is that journalism is unreadable and literature is not read.

OSCAR WILDE

There's nothing to writing. All you do is sit down at a type-writer and open a vein.
RED SMITH

We romantic writers are there to make people feel and not think. A historical romance is the only kind of book where chastity really counts.
BARBARA CARTLAND

To read a group of novels these days is a depressing experi-ence. After the fourth or fifth, I find myself thinking about 'The Novel' and I feel a desperate desire to sneak out to a movie.
LESLIE FIEDLER

I think you must remember that a writer is a simple-minded person to begin with and go on that basis. He's not a great mind, he's not a great thinker, he's not a great philosopher, he's a storyteller.
ERSKINE CALDWELL

Immature artists imitate. Mature artists steal.
LIONEL TRILLING

When a thing has been said, and well said, have no scruple: take it and copy it.
ANATOLE FRANCE

Remember why the good Lord made your eyes, Pla-gi-a-rize!
TOM LEHRER

If you copy from one author it's plagiarism. If you copy from two, it's research.

WILSON MIZNER

Next o'er his books his eyes began to roll,
In pleasing memory of all he stole.

ALEXANDER POPE

Just get it down on paper, and then we'll see what to do with it.

MAXWELL PERKINS' *advice to Marcia Davenport*

Never make excuses, never let them see you bleed, and never get separated from your baggage.

WESLEY PRICE, *"Three Rules of Professional Comportment for Writers"*

Writing is for the most part a lonely and unsatisfying occupation. One is tied to a table, a chair, a stack of paper.

GRAHAM GREENE

When I am working on a book or a story I write every morning as soon after the first light as possible. There is no one to disturb you and it is cool or cold and you come to your work and warm as you write.

ERNEST HEMINGWAY

Rome had as many as forty libraries operating during its imperial period, along with a lively book trade... works came directly into the shop from authors and were handed over to the scribes, and copies were produced.

NICHOLAS A. BASBANES, *in A Gentle Madness*

The tools I need for my work are paper, tobacco, food, and a little whiskey.

WILLIAM FAULKNER

The ideal view for daily writing, hour on hour, is the blank brick wall of a cold-storage warehouse. Failing this, a stretch of sky will do, cloudless if possible.

EDNA FERBER

The perfect place for a writer is in the hideous roar of a city, with men making a new road under his window in competition with a barrel organ, and on the mat a man waiting for the rent.

HENRY VOLLAM MORTON

Writing is a solitary occupation. Family, friends, and society are the natural enemies of a writer. He must be alone, uninterrupted, and slightly savage if he is to sustain and complete an undertaking.

LAWRENCE CLARK POWELL

I felt like you can write forever, but you have a short time to raise a family. And I think a family is a lot more important than writing.

KEN KESEY

All my major works have been written in prison.... I would recommend prison not only to aspiring writers but to aspiring politicians, too.

JAWAHARLAL NEHRU

The best time for planning a book is while you're doing the dishes.

AGATHA CHRISTIE

What no wife of a writer can ever understand is that a writer is working when he's staring out of the window.

BURTON RASCOE

Often while reading a book one feels that the author would have preferred to paint rather than write; one can sense the pleasure he derives from describing a landscape or a person, as if he were painting what he is saying, because deep in his heart he would have preferred to use brushes and colors.

PABLO PICASSO

Writing is a form of therapy; sometimes I wonder how all those who do not write, compose or paint can manage to escape the madness, the melancholia, the panic fear which is inherent in a human situation.

GRAHAM GREENE

The man of letters loves not only to be read but to be seen. Happy to be by himself, he would be happier still if people knew that he was happy to be by himself, working in solitude at night under his lamp.

REMY DE GOURMONT

If I could I would always work in silence and obscurity, and let my efforts be known by their results.

EMILY BRONTE

Only ambitious nonentities and hearty mediocrities exhibit their rough drafts. It is like passing around samples of one's sputum.

VLADIMIR NABOKOV

I just think it's bad to talk about one's present work, for it spoils something at the root of the creative act. It discharges the tension.

NORMAN MAILER

Mostly, we authors must repeat ourselves—that's the truth. We have two or three great moving experiences in our lives—experiences so great and moving that it doesn't seem at the time that anyone else has been caught up and pounded and dazzled and astonished and beaten and broken and rescued and illuminated and rewarded and humbled in just that way ever before.

F. SCOTT FITZGERALD

I think that in order to write really well and convincingly, one must be somewhat poisoned by emotion. Dislike, displeasure, resentment, fault-finding, imagination, passionate remonstrance, a sense of injustice—they all make fine fuel.

EDNA FERBER

I wrote the scenes... by using the same apprehensive imagination that occurs in the morning before an afternoon's appointment with my dentist.

JOHN MARQUAND

I've always believed in writing without a collaborator, because where two people are writing the same book, each believes he gets all the worries and only half the royalties.

AGATHA CHRISTIE

I never could understand how two men can write a book together; to me that's like three people getting together to have a baby.

EVELYN WAUGH

Why do people always expect authors to answer questions? I am an author because I want to ask questions. If I had answers I'd be a politician.

EUGENE IONESCO

INTERVIEWER: How many drafts of a story do you do?
S. J. PERELMAN: Thirty-seven. I once tried doing thirty-three, but something was lacking, a certain—how shall I say?—je ne sais quoi. On another occasion, I tried forty-two versions, but the final effect was too lapidary—you know what I mean, Jack? What the hell are you trying to extort—my trade secrets?

People who read me seem to be divided into four groups: twenty-five percent like me for the right reasons; twenty-five percent like me for the wrong reasons; twenty-five percent hate me for the wrong reasons; twenty-five percent hate me for the right reasons. It's that last twenty-five percent that worries me.

ROBERT FROST

An author ought to write for the youth of his own generation, the critics of the next, and the schoolmasters of ever afterwards.

F. SCOTT FITZGERALD

When I want to read a good book, I write one.

BENJAMIN DISRAELI

I can't understand why a person will take a year to write a novel when he can easily buy one for a few dollars.

FRED ALLEN

Only when one has lost all curiosity about the future has one reached the age to write an autobiography.
EVELYN WAUGH

And because I found I had nothing else to write about, I presented myself as a subject.
MONTAIGNE

I'll be eighty this month. Age, if nothing else, entitles me to set the record straight before I dissolve. I've given my memoirs far more thought than any of my marriages. You can't divorce a book.
GLORIA SWANSON

A well-written life is almost as rare as a well-spent one.
THOMAS CARLYLE

How can one make a life out of six cardboard boxes full of tailors' bills, love letters and old picture postcards?
VIRGINIA WOOLF

A novelist, in his omniscience, knows the measure of his characters, out of his passion for all sorts of conditions of human life. The biographer, however, begins with certain limiting little facts.
LEON EDEL

On the trail of another man, the biographer must put up with finding himself at every turn: any biography uneasily shelters an autobiography within it.
PAUL MURRAY KENDALL

The novel is the highest example of subtle interrelatedness that man has discovered.

D.H. LAWRENCE

As a fiction writer I find it convenient not to believe things. Not to disbelieve them either, just move them into a realm where everything is held in suspension.

WILLIAM GASS

What makes a good writer of history is a guy who is suspicious. Suspicion marks the real difference between the man who wants to write honest history and the one who'd rather write a good story.

JIM BISHOP

People need books with an epic background. They are bored with books that tell only one story on one level. They need something fantastic, something that gives them a sense of living in history. As it is, most novels aren't giving readers a chance to use their sense of history.

GÜNTER GRASS

Everyone who works in the domain of fiction is a bit crazy. The problem is to render this craziness interesting.

FRANCOIS TRUFFAUT

Every author really wants to have letters printed in the papers. Unable to make the grade, he drops down a rung of the ladder and writes novels.

P.G. WODEHOUSE

I have never met an author who admitted that people did not buy his book because it was dull.

W. SOMERSET MAUGHAM

Prose books are the show dogs I breed and sell to support my cat.

ROBERT GRAVES, *on writing novels to support his love of writing poetry*

The value of great fiction, we begin to suspect, is not that it entertains us or distracts us from our troubles, not just that it broadens our knowledge of people and places, but also that it helps us to know what we believe, reinforces the qualities that are noblest in us, leads us to feel uneasy about our failures and limitations.

JOHN GARDNER

When audiences come to see us authors lecture, it is largely in the hope that we'll be funnier to look at than to read.

SINCLAIR LEWIS

A writer is congenitally unable to tell the truth and that is why we call what he writes fiction.

WILLIAM FAULKNER

How pleasant it is to respect people! When I see books, I am not concerned with how the authors loved or played cards; I see only their marvellous works.

ANTON CHEKHOV

Writers seldom choose as friends those self-contained characters who are never in trouble, never unhappy or ill, never make mistakes, and always count their change when it is handed to them.

CATHERINE DRINKER BOWEN

There is only one trait that marks the writer. He is always watching. It's a kind of trick of the mind and he is born with it.

MORLEY CALLAGHAN

In any work that is truly creative, I believe, the writer cannot be omniscient in advance about the effects that he proposes to produce. The suspense of a novel is not only in the reader, but in the novelist, who is intensely curious about what will happen to the hero.

MARY McCARTHY

How can you write if you can't cry?

RING LARDNER

Writing a book is a horrible, exhausting struggle, like a long bout of some painful illness. One would never undertake such a thing if one were not driven by some demon whom one can neither resist nor understand.

GEORGE ORWELL

They're fancy talkers about themselves, writers. If I had to give young writers advice, I would say don't listen to writers talk about writing or themselves.

LILLIAN HELLMAN

Advice to young writers? Always the same advice: learn to trust your own judgment, learn inner independence, learn to trust that time will sort the good from the bad—including your own bad.

DORIS LESSING

Most writers, you know, are awful sticks to talk with.

SHERWOOD ANDERSON

Writers seldom wish other writers well.

SAUL BELLOW

What a heartbreaking job it is trying to combine authors for their own protection! I had ten years of it on the Committee of Management of the Society of Authors; and the first lesson I learned was that when you take the field for the authors you will be safer without a breastplate than without a backplate.

GEORGE BERNARD SHAW

If I didn't know the ending of a story, I wouldn't begin. I always write my last line, my last paragraph, my last page first.

KATHERINE ANNE PORTER

Writing every book is like a purge; at the end of it one is empty... like a dry shell on the beach, waiting for the tide to come in again.

DAPHNE DU MAURIER

....

We need not worry much about writers. Man will always find a means to gratify a passion. He will write, as he commits adultery, in spite of taxation.

GRAHAM GREENE

I can always find plenty of women to sleep with but the kind of woman that is really hard for me to find is a typist who can read my writing.

THOMAS WOLFE

One hates an author that's all author.

LORD BYRON

Your manuscript is both good and original; but the part that is good is not original, and the part that is original is not good.

SAMUEL JOHNSON

Manuscript: something submitted in haste and returned at leisure.

OLIVER HERFORD

I've never signed a contract, so never have a deadline. A deadline's an unnerving thing. I just finish a book, and if the publisher doesn't like it that's his privilege. There've been many, many rejections. If you want to write it your own way, that's the chance you take.

MARCHETTE CHUTE

We have read your manuscript with boundless delight. If we were to publish your paper, it would be impossible for us to publish any work of lower standard. And as it is unthinkable that in the next thousand years we shall see its equal, we are, to our regret, compelled to return your divine composition, and to beg you a thousand times to overlook our short sight and timidity.

> REJECTION SLIP FROM A CHINESE ECONOMIC
> JOURNAL, *quoted in the Financial Times.*

The first thing an unpublished author should remember is that no one asked him to write in the first place. With this firmly in mind, he has no right to become discouraged just because other people are being published.

> JOHN FARRAR

Only a small minority of authors over-write themselves. Most of the good and the tolerable ones do not write enough.

> ARNOLD BENNETT

The faster I write the better my output. If I'm going slow I'm in trouble. It means I'm pushing the words instead of being pulled by them.

> RAYMOND CHANDLER

With sixty staring me in the face, I have developed inflammation of the sentence structure and a definite hardening of the paragraphs.

> JAMES THURBER, *at age 59*

A collection of short stories is generally thought to be a horrendous clinker; an enforced courtesy for the elderly writer who wants to display the trophies of his youth, along with his trout flies.

JOHN CHEEVER

I finished my first book seventy-six years ago. I offered it to every publisher on the English-speaking earth I had ever heard of. Their refusals were unanimous: and it did not get into print until, fifty years later, publishers would publish anything that had my name on it.

GEORGE BERNARD SHAW

Literary success of any enduring kind is made by refusing to do what publishers want, by refusing to write what the public wants, by refusing to accept any popular standard, by refusing to write anything to order.

LAFCADIO HEARN

A book must be done according to the writer's conception of it as nearly perfect as possible, and the publishing problems begin then. That is, the publisher must not try to get a writer to fit the book to the conditions of the trade, etc. It must be the other way around.

MAXWELL PERKINS

At least half the mystery novels published violate the law that the solution, once revealed, must seem to be inevitable.

RAYMOND CHANDLER

The crown of literature is poetry. It is its end and aim. It is the sublimest activity of the human mind. It is the achievement of beauty and delicacy. The writer of prose can only step aside when the poet passes.

W. SOMERSET MAUGHAM

Everybody has their own idea of what's a poet. Robert Frost, President Johnson, T.S. Eliot, Rudolf Valentino—they're all poets. I like to think of myself as the one who carries the light bulb.

BOB DYLAN

Women have always been poor, not for two hundred years merely, but from the beginning of time... Women, then, have not had a dog's chance of writing poetry. That is why I have laid so much stress on money and a room of one's own.

VIRGINIA WOOLF

I love you sons of bitches. You're the only ones with guts enough to really care about the future, who really notice what machines do to us, what wars do to us, what cities do to us, what tremendous misunderstandings, mistakes, accidents, and catastrophes do to us. You're the only ones zany enough to agonize over time and distances without limit, over mysteries that will never die, over the fact that we are right now determining whether the space voyage for the next billion years or so is going to be Heaven or Hell.

THE DRUNKEN HERO *in Kurt Vonnegut's God Bless You, Mr. Rosewater, who blunders into a convention of science fiction writers*

You don't have to suffer to be a poet. Adolescence is enough suffering for anyone.

JOHN CIARDI

The poet, as everyone knows, must strike his individual note sometime between the ages of fifteen and twenty-five. He may hold it a long time, or a short time, but it is then he must strike it or never. School and college have been conducted with the almost express purpose of keeping him busy with something else till the danger of his ever creating anything has past.

ROBERT FROST

Great poetry is always written by somebody straining to go beyond what he can do.

STEPHEN SPENDER

To have written one good poem—good used seriously—is an unlikely and marvelous thing that only a couple hundred of writers of English, at the most, have done—it's like sitting out in the yard in the evening and having a meteorite fall in one's lap.

RANDALL JARRELL

It's silly to suggest the writing of poetry as something ethereal, a sort of soul-crashing emotional experience that wrings you. I have no fancy ideas about poetry. It doesn't come to you on the wings of a dove. It's something you work hard at.

LOUISE BOGAN

If I feel physically as if the top of my head were taken off,
I know that is poetry.
EMILY DICKINSON

I was too slow a mover. It was much easier to be a poet.
T. S. ELIOT *on giving up boxing in college*

I could no more define poetry than a terrier can define a rat.
A.E. HOUSMAN

I believe that every English poet should read the English
classics, master the rules of grammar before he attempts to
bend or break them, travel abroad, experience the horrors
of sordid passion, and—if he is lucky enough—know the
love of an honest woman.
ROBERT GRAVES

Were poets to be suppressed, my friends, with no history,
no ancient lays, save that each had a father, nothing of any
man would be heard hereafter.
GIOLLA BRIGHDE MHAC CON MIDH *(circa 1259)*

Let every eye negotiate for itself, and trust no agent.
WILLIAM SHAKESPEARE

The job of editor in a publishing house is the dullest, hardest, most exciting, exasperating and rewarding of perhaps
any job in the world.
JOHN HALL WHEELOCK

Most editors generally can't recognize bad writing when they read it. Nor do they try very hard to learn to recognize it.
ALFRED KNOPF

Listen carefully to first criticisms of your work. Note just what it is about your work that the critics don't like—then cultivate it. That's the part of your work that's individual and worth keeping.
JEAN COCTEAU

Nine out of ten writers, I am sure, could write more. I think they should and, if they did, they would find their work improving even beyond their own, their agent's and their editor's highest hopes.
JOHN CREASEY

No passion in the world is equal to the passion to alter someone else's draft.
H.G. WELLS

Great editors do not discover nor produce great authors; great authors create and produce great publishers.
JOHN FARRAR